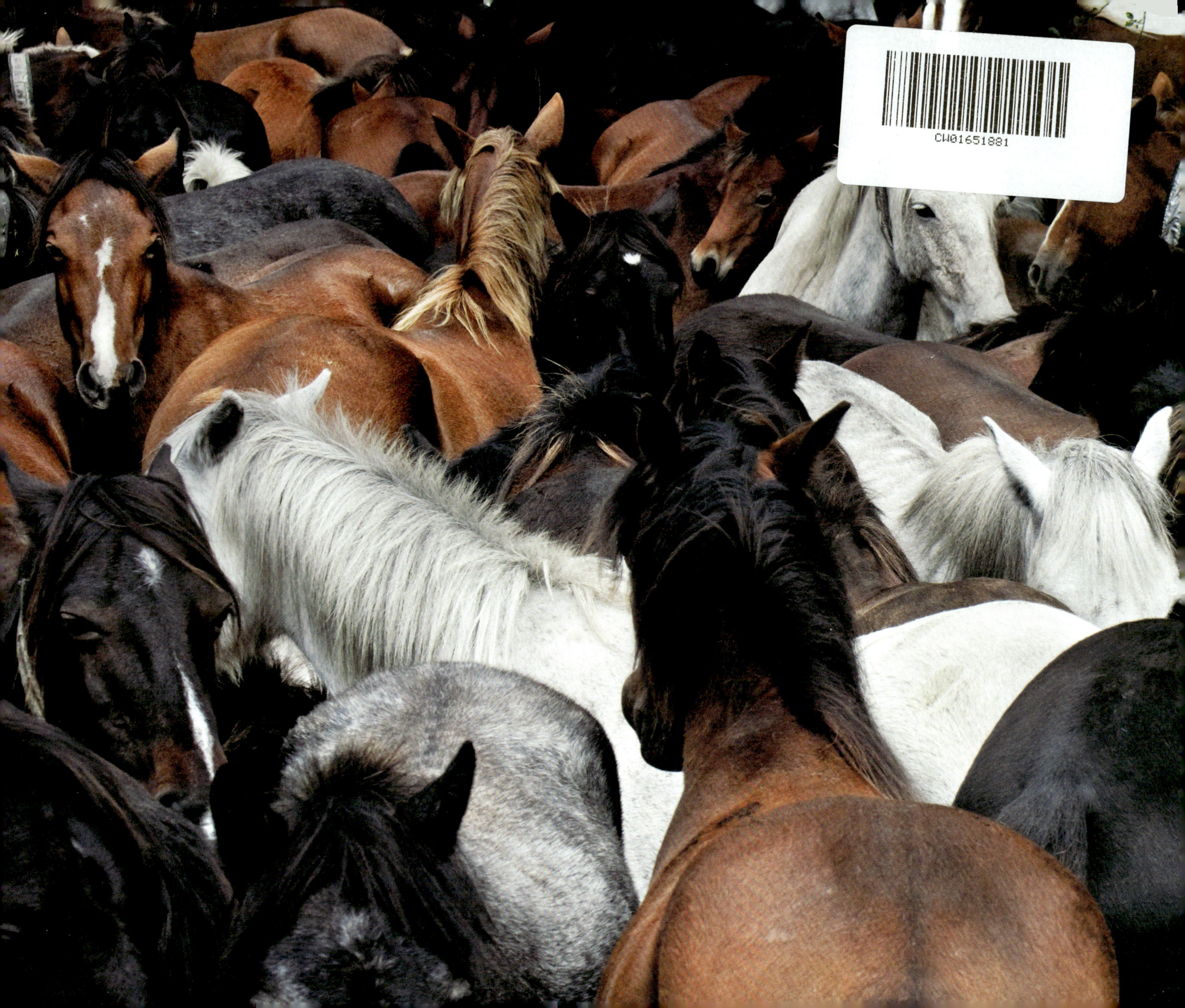

First published in 2009
by Tile Barn Farm
Brockenhurst,
Hampshire,
SO42 7UF

www.tilebarnfarm.com

A CIP catalogue record for this book is available from the British Library.

ISBN 978-0-9562643-0-5
Printed by EBS, Italy

Design by SMITH®
Victoria Forrest, Lesley Gilmour
www.smith-design.com

Front cover Ray Readhead's New Forest ponies grazing at Beaulieu.
Back cover Commonor with his sow near Rufus Stone. New Forest, 1906. Photographer unknown.
Previous A successful drift for Agister Robert Maton who together with his commoners brought in a record 257 ponies on the Latchmoor drift, 2008.

For Richard with love

The Commoners' **New Forest**

It is an arduous job going out
to see what has happened to your
animals. The commoners do it
for love.

For The Parkers

Sally Fear

May 2019

by Sally Fear

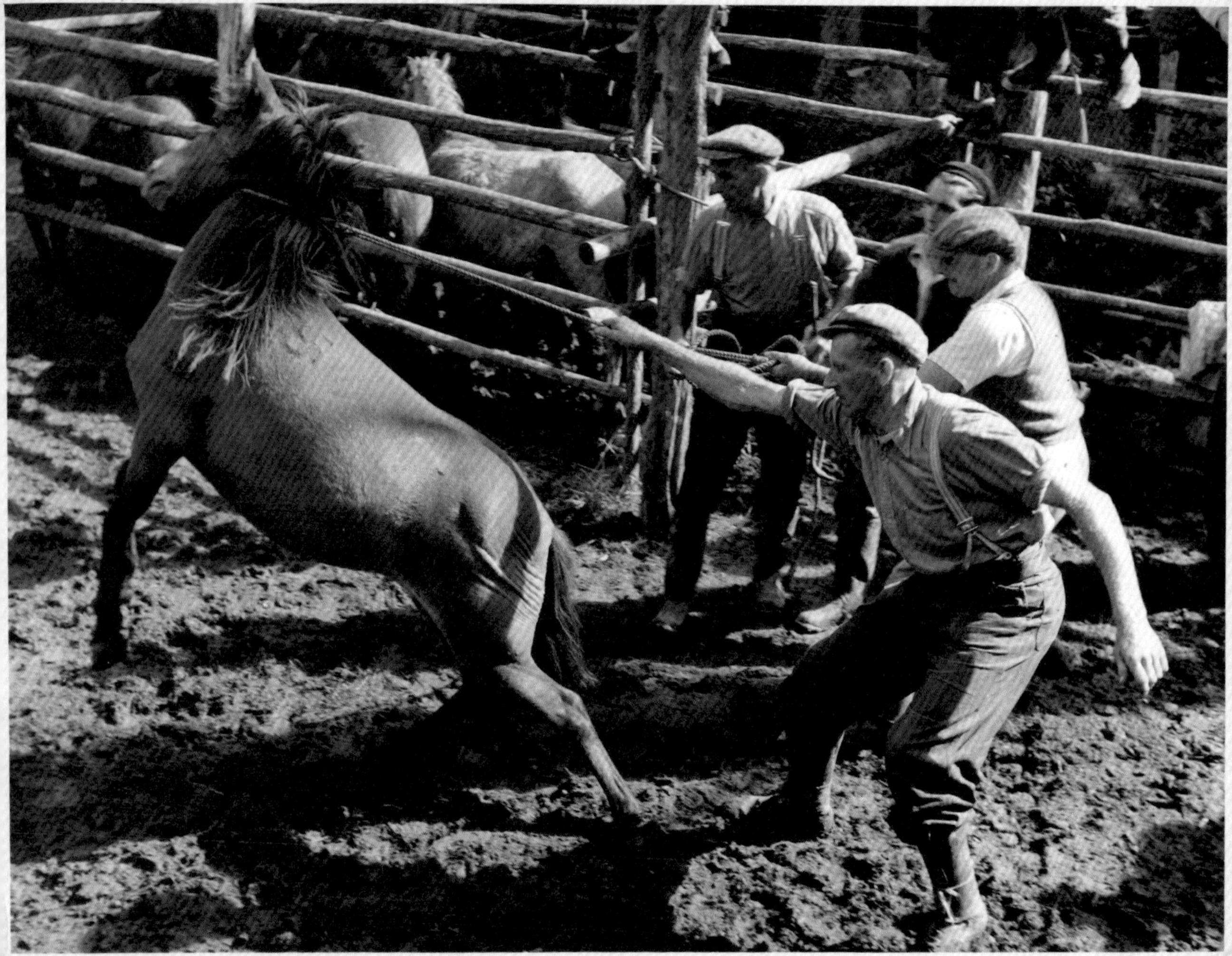

New Forest Commoners' Defence Association 1909–2009

This book is a celebration of the Centenary of the New Forest Commoners' Defence Association and its members—the commoners. The next few pages of photographs show New Forest commoners during the past century.

The following is extracted from the obituary in the New Forest Commoners' Defence fourth Annual Report in the year 1913:

> All Commoners and especially the Members of this Association received the news of the sad event of the death of Lord Arthur Cecil, 1851–1913, with deepest regret, and it cast a deep gloom over them, having lost their Chairman, who was always the New Forest Commoners' Champion, Defender and Friend, his life in the Forest providing this by his having always adhered to their rights. His valuable work for them will never be forgotten, or his services which were ever at their disposal.
>
> Lord Arthur Cecil was the founder of this Association, when on the 14th January, 1909, he called a Public Meeting of all Commoners at Brockenhurst, when in explaining the object of the Meeting, he said it was to bind themselves together for the Defence, and not the Offence of their rights as Commoners of the New Forest. He had long wished to form an Association, to which Members could subscribe a small amount, to assist any Member, especially the small Commoner, from having to pay excessive Poundage charges, etc., by defending their case, and by having gates erected; and this he carried out up to the time of his death.

It is important to realise that many of those names in the 1909 list of subscribers to the New Forest Commoners' Defence Association are still listed as members of the NFCDA today. Names like Drodge, Kitcher, Penny, Stride—still in the same village—and sometimes still in the same house or holding. A commoner's roots are very important and there can be few places in Britain that have such a concentration of family lines. Some consider the commoners' Forest traditions as from a bygone era, but they make the Forest what it is today—unique.

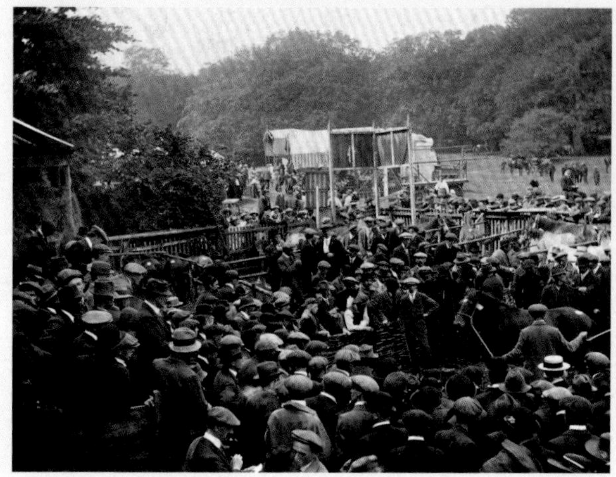

Opposite The greatly respected Don Stephens 1921-2007, a true 'Forest man' seen handling a colt at Crabhat pound with Charlie Dovey and on their right Bob Kitcher, circa 1950. Photographer Thomas A Wilkie.
Above Lyndhurst Fair at Swan Green, 1912.

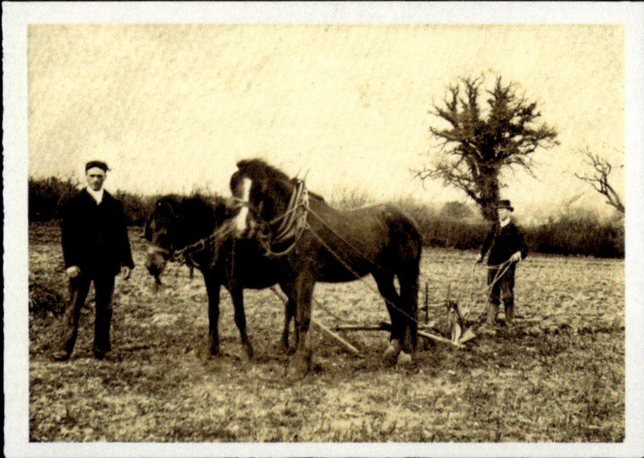

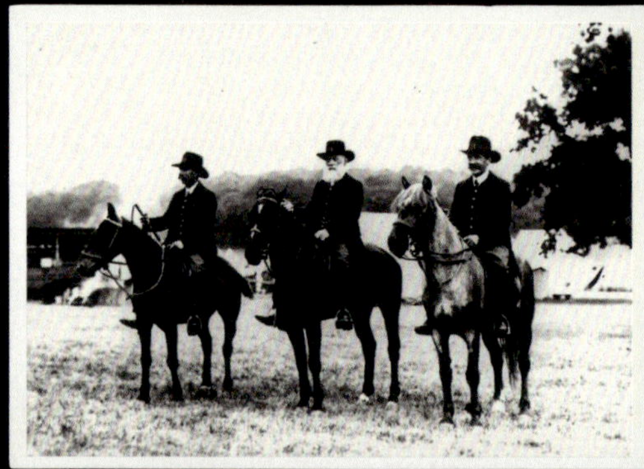

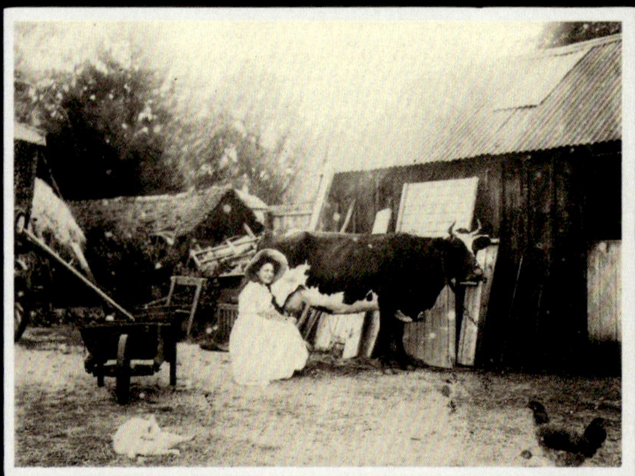

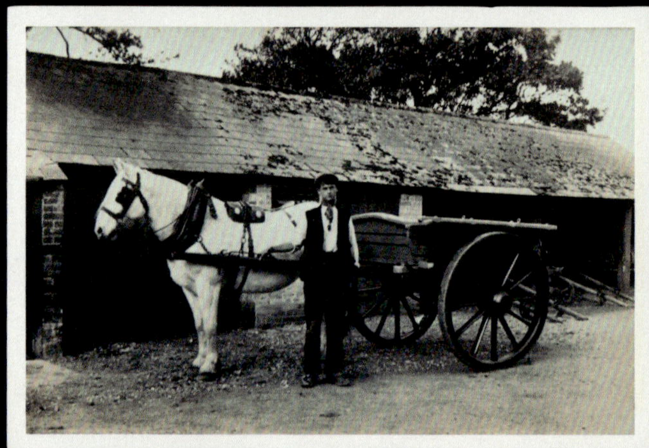

Above (clockwise from top-left) Frank Drodge and Frank Drodge, circa 1920; Agisters Albert Evemy, Charles Evemy and Jesse Taylor at Godshill Camp, 1910; George Gregory (great grandfather of Jonathan Gerrelli), circa 1900; Milking in the stack yard, Oak Tree Farm, Exbury, 1903.

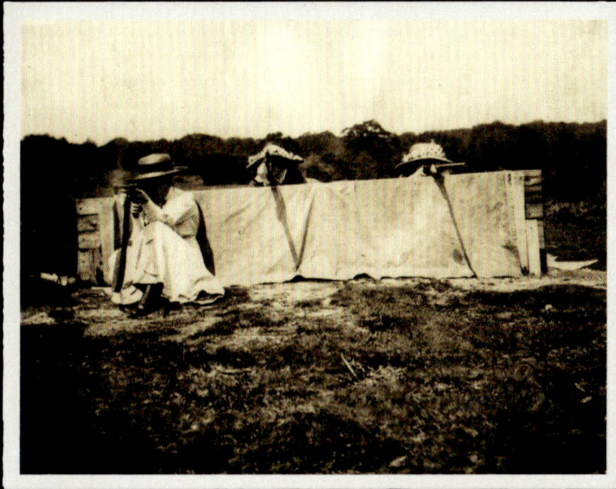

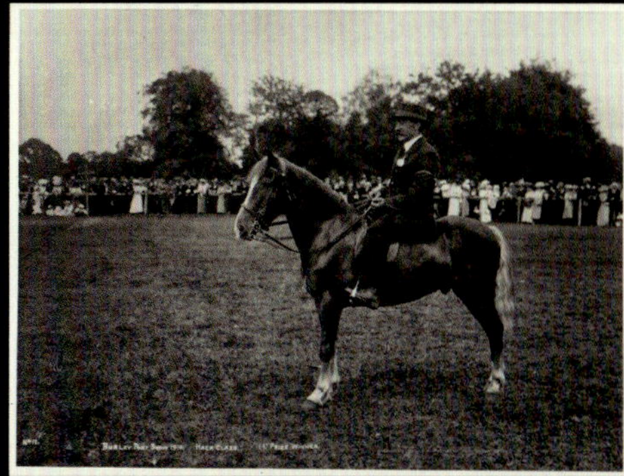
BURLEY PONY SHOW
HACK CLASS
1st PRIZE WINNER

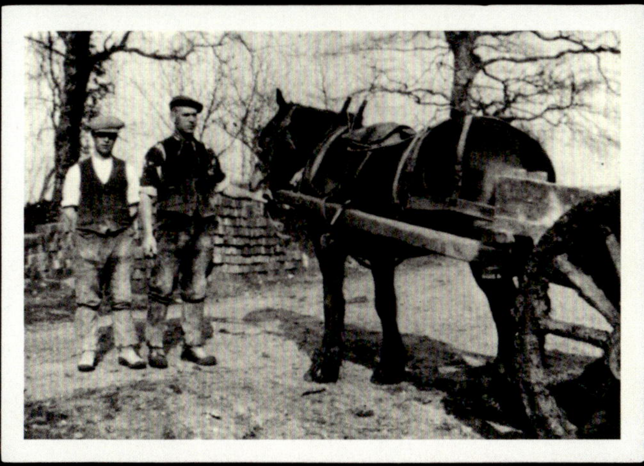

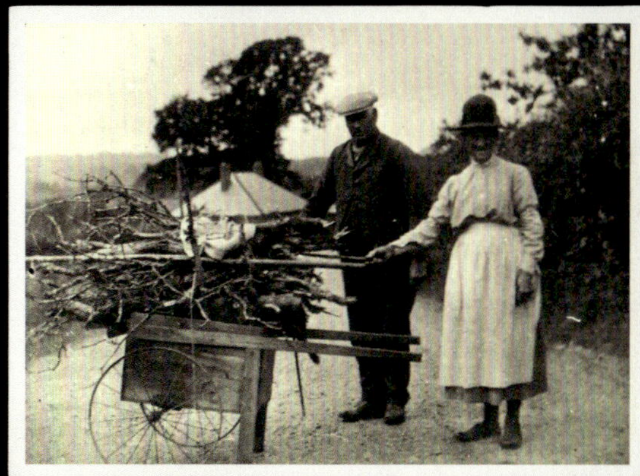

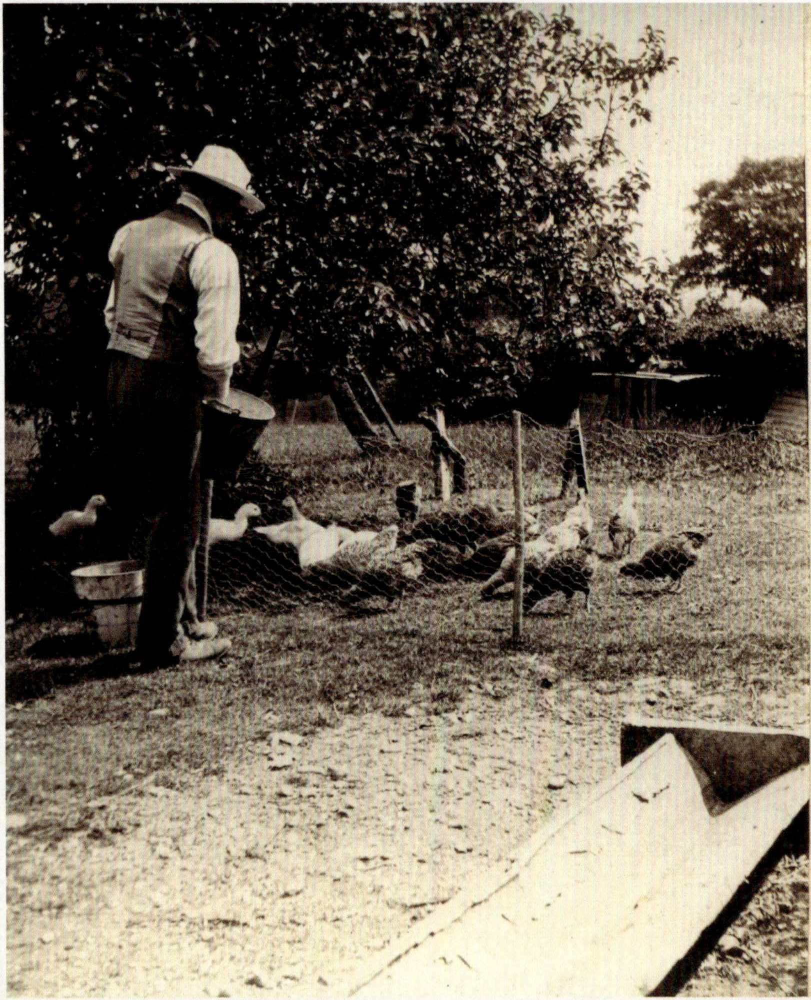

Near Lyndhurst. New Forest.
June 1906

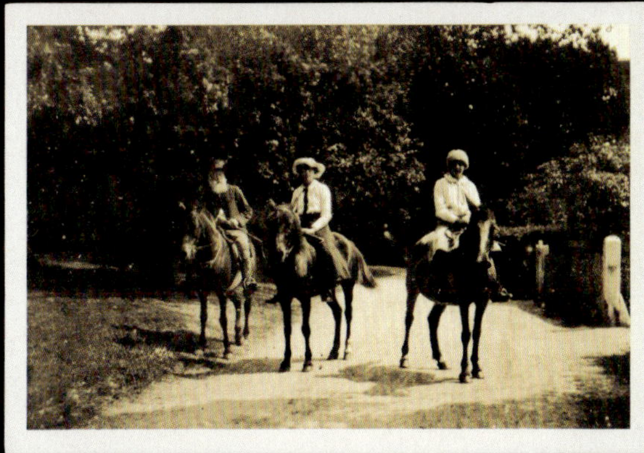

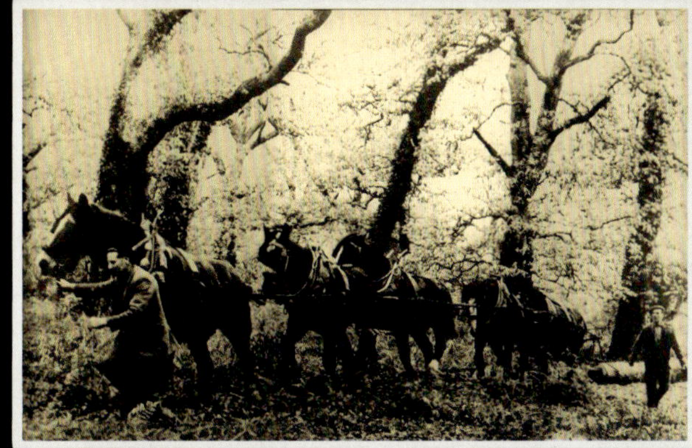

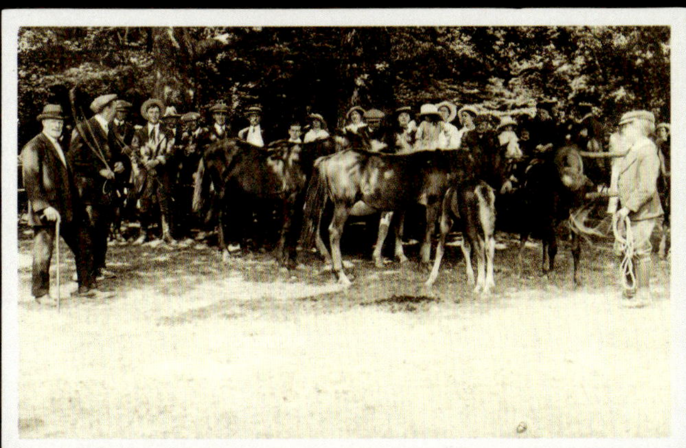

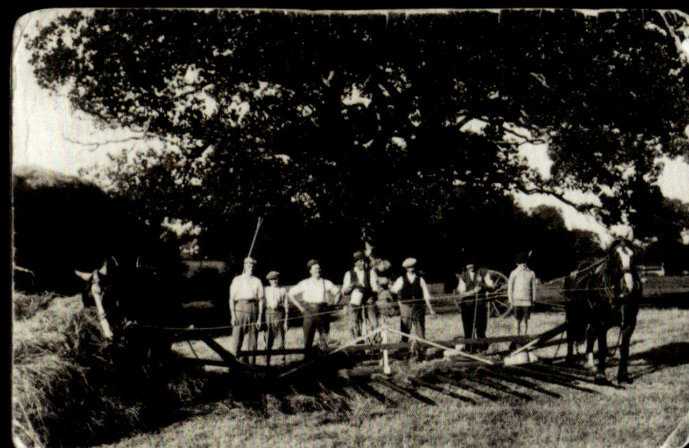

Above (clockwise from top-left) Agister Charles Evemy on Blacky, Ruth Dent on Deborah and Iris Rider on Roany, 1899; Jim Witt (left) and Bob Kitcher (right) with horse team Duke, Jack, Jolly, Blossom and Madal, circa 1950; First hay sweep machine in the Forest, (left to right) Duke Street, Alfie Smith, Charles Penny, George Bright, Bob Allen, Riley Collins, Freddy Bright and horses Colonel and Flower, 1928; George Henry Penny (far left) at the Swan Green Fair, circa 1900.

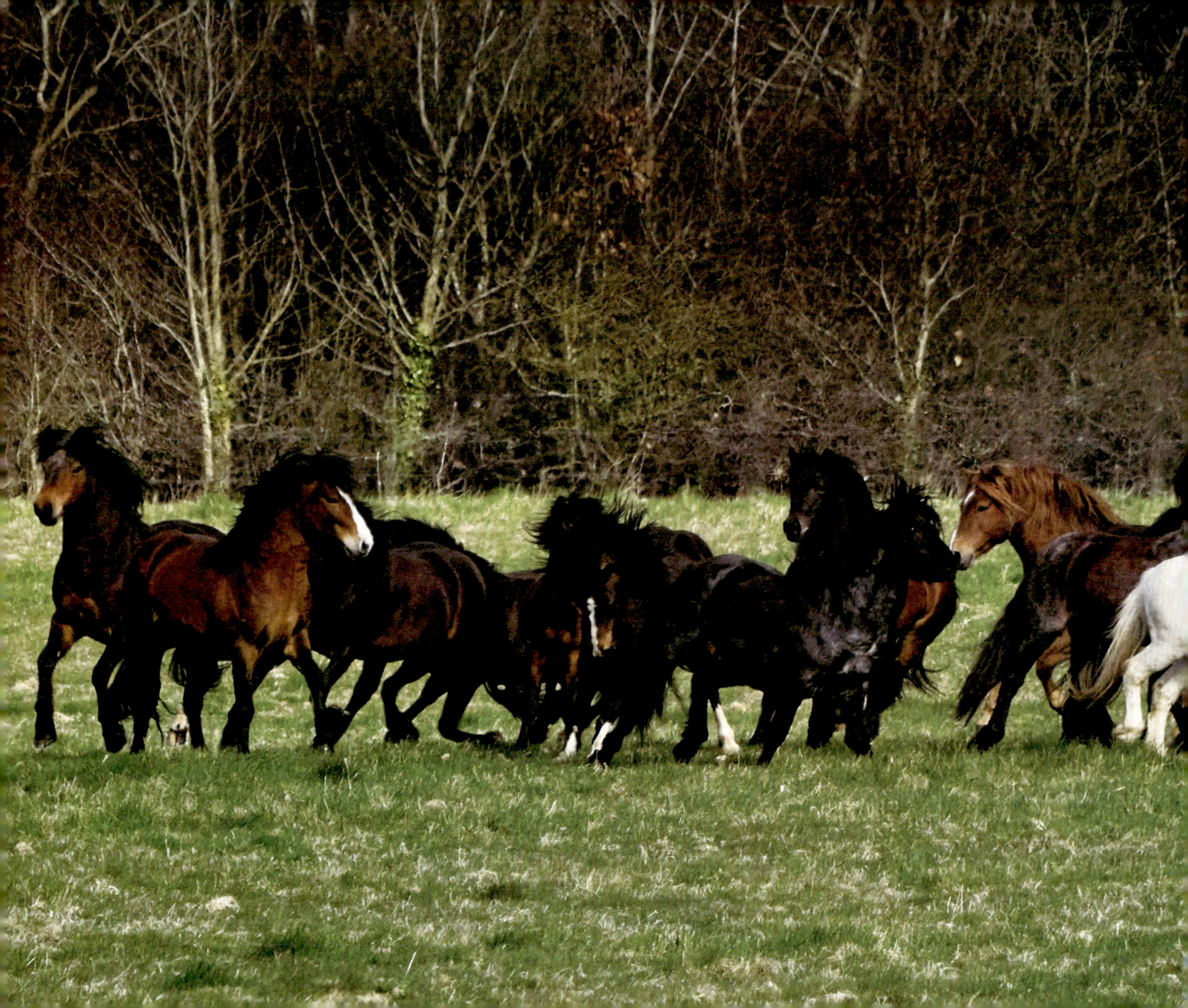

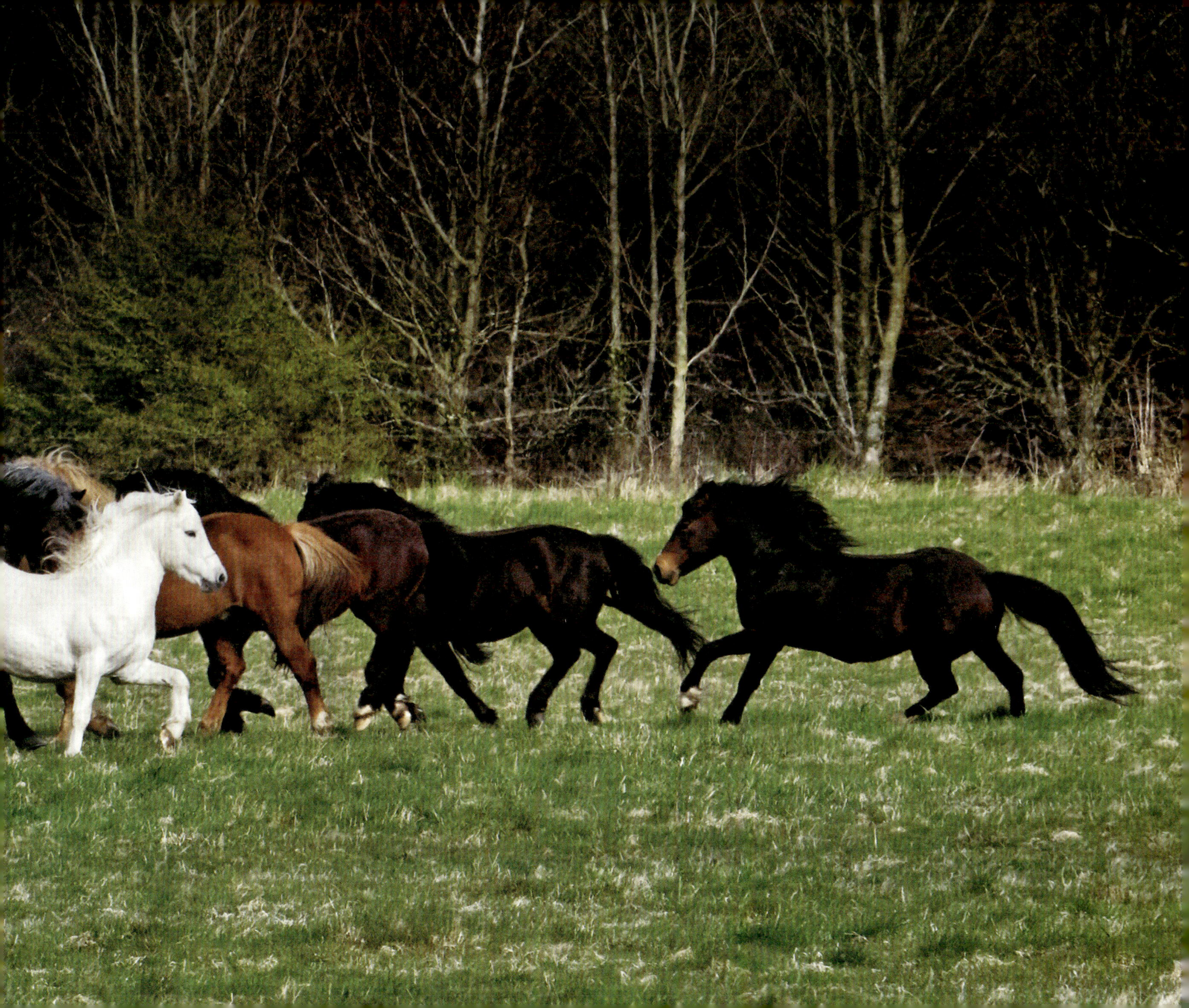

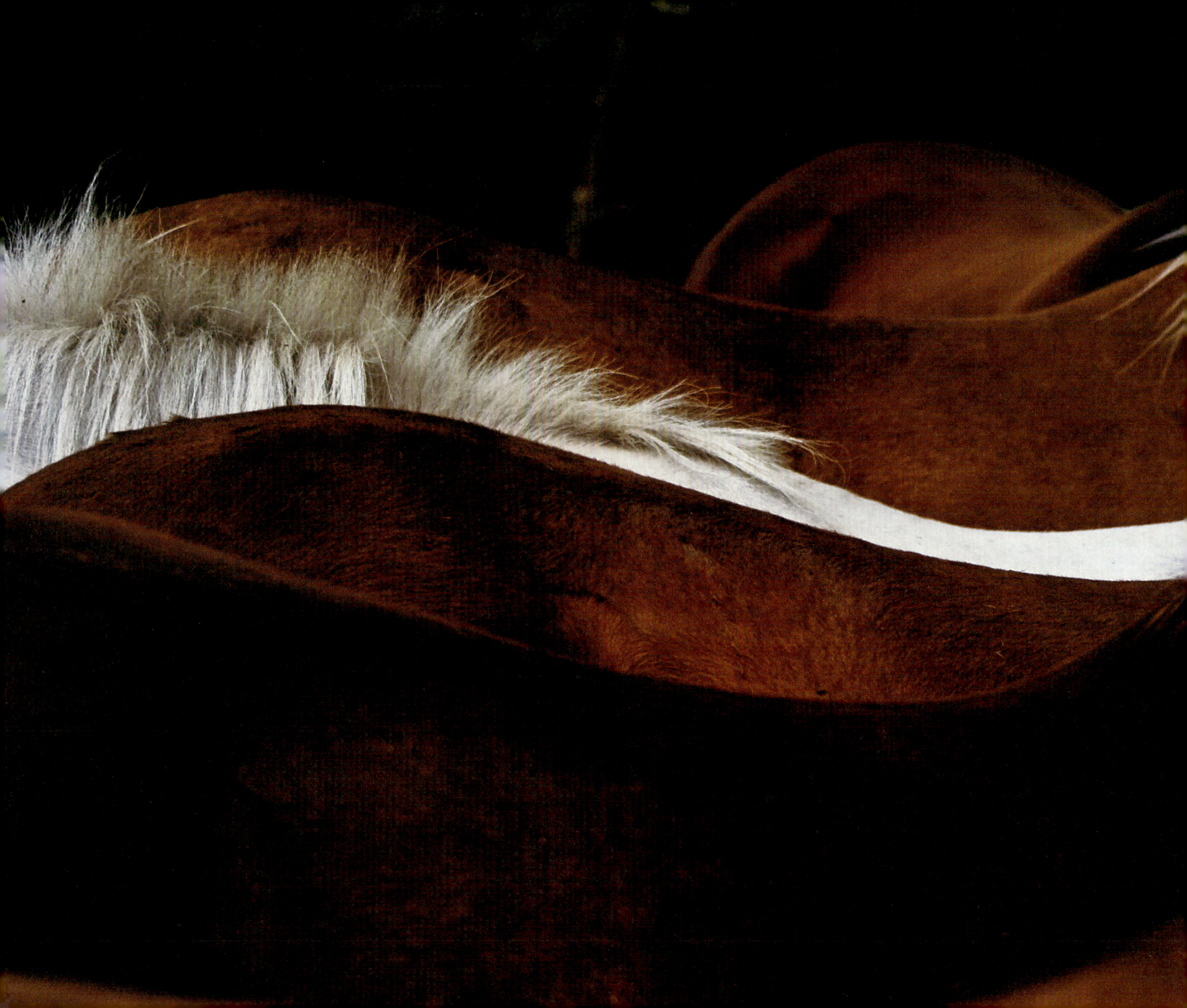

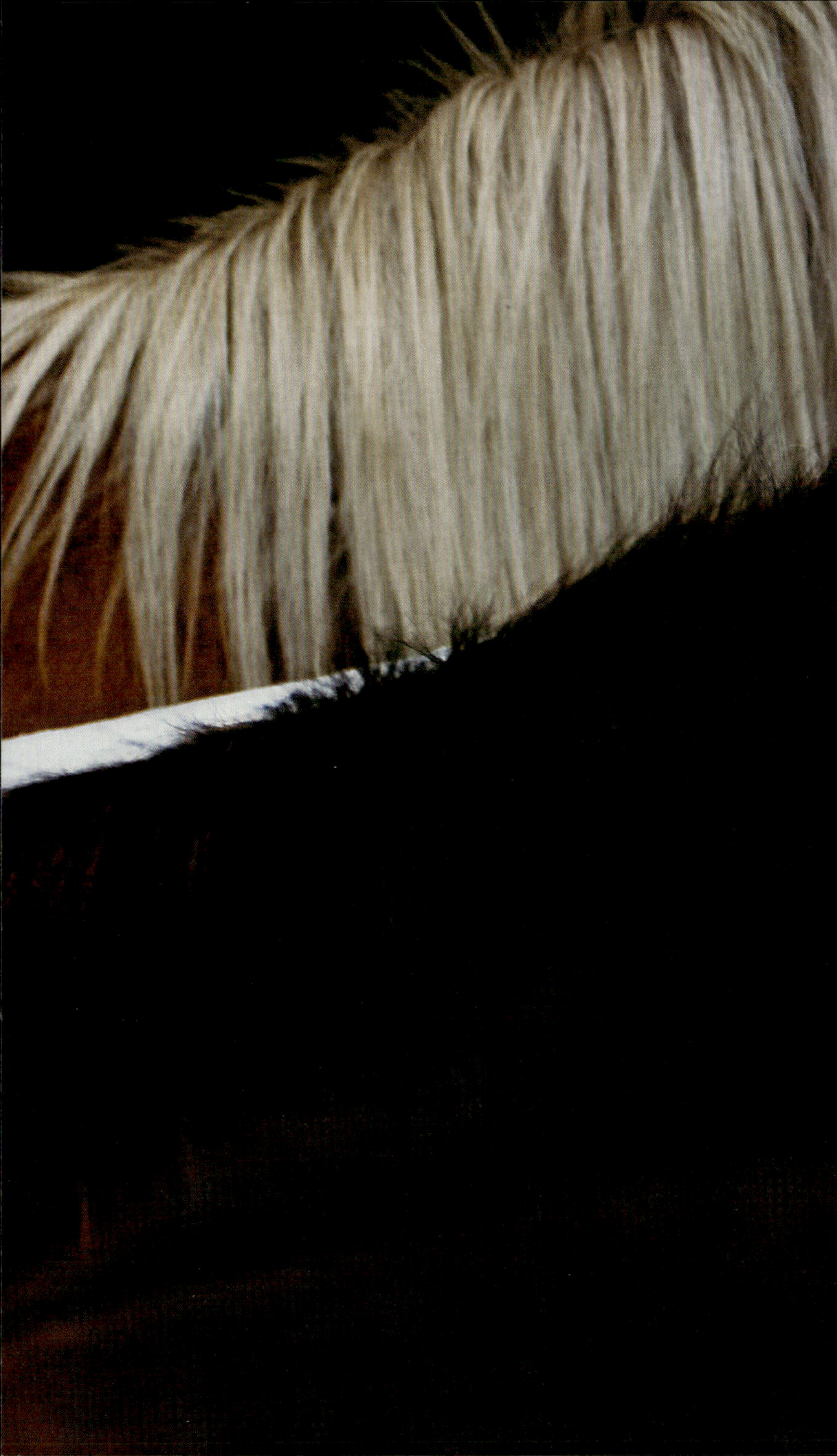

Contents

Previous New Forest Stallions on their winter grazing, Cadland Estate, 2009.
Opposite New Forest Ponies in the pound at Ipley, 2008.

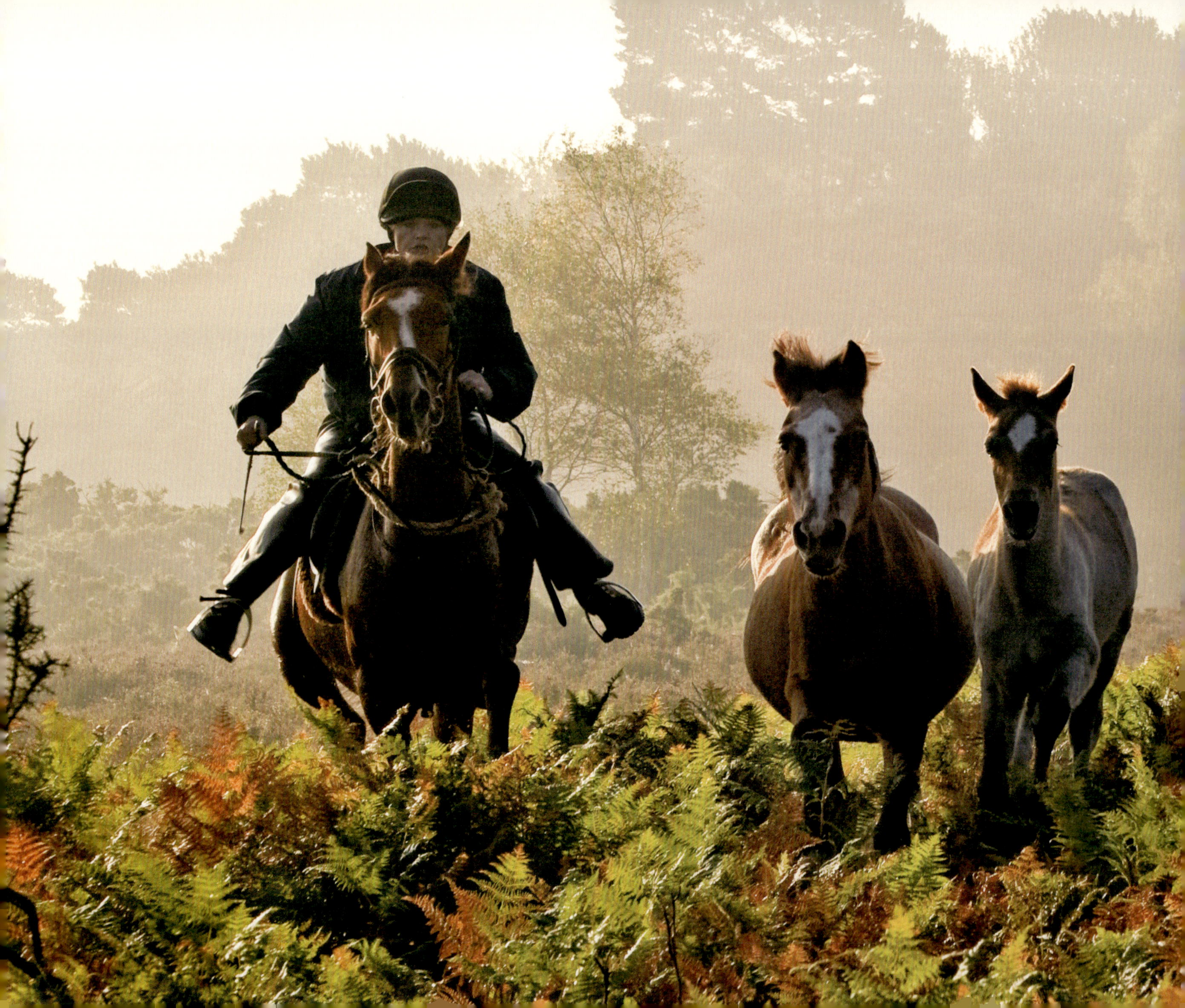

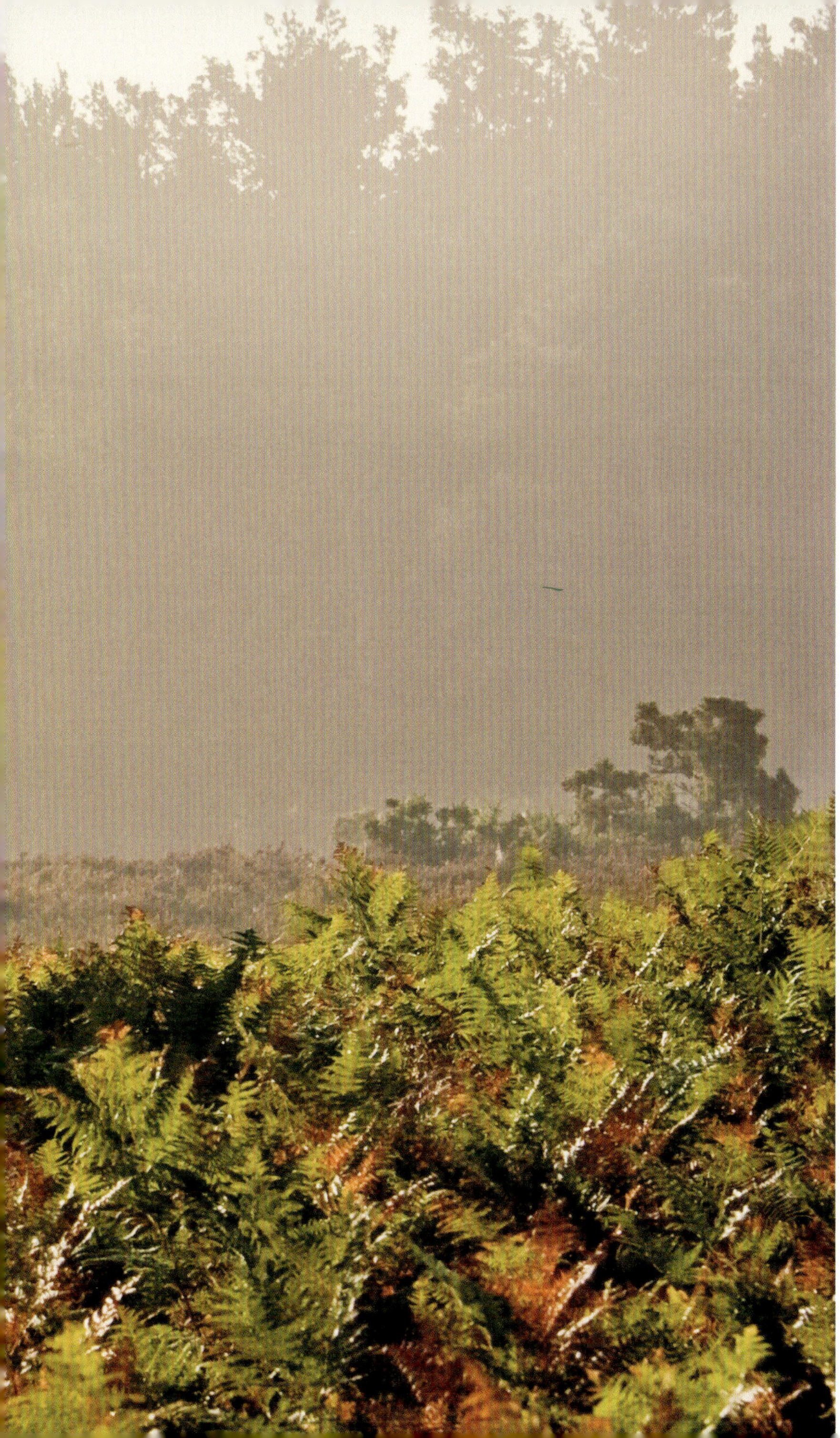

Foreword

The title of this small book is very apt since it reminds us all that the New Forest is the creation of almost a thousand years of constant agricultural use by generations of local families.

Without the commoners and their animals the Forest would not exist. The preservation of this unique landscape entirely depends upon the continued practice of these ancient rights of common.

Sally Fear's excellent collection of photographs is a valuable and stirring way of not letting us forget that if we wish to preserve the New Forest we must understand, support and if necessary defend these traditions, the Forest's future depends on it.

Oliver Crosthwaite Eyre, Official Verderer

Autumn morning on Culverley, Lucinda Ingram bringing in her neighbour Anne Keller's mare Fiddlers Stella and foal Fiddlers Sonny Jim for weaning and branding, 2007.

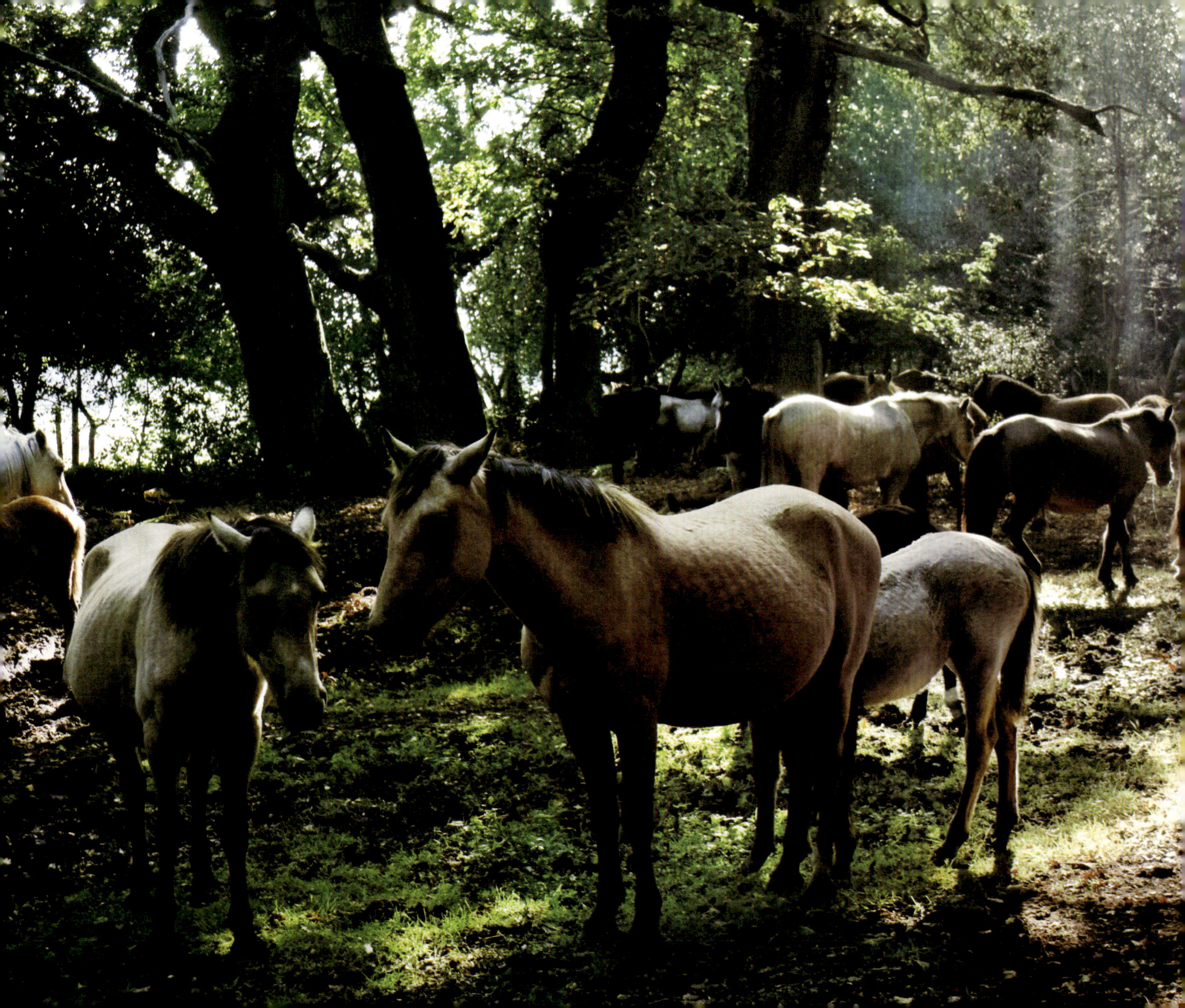

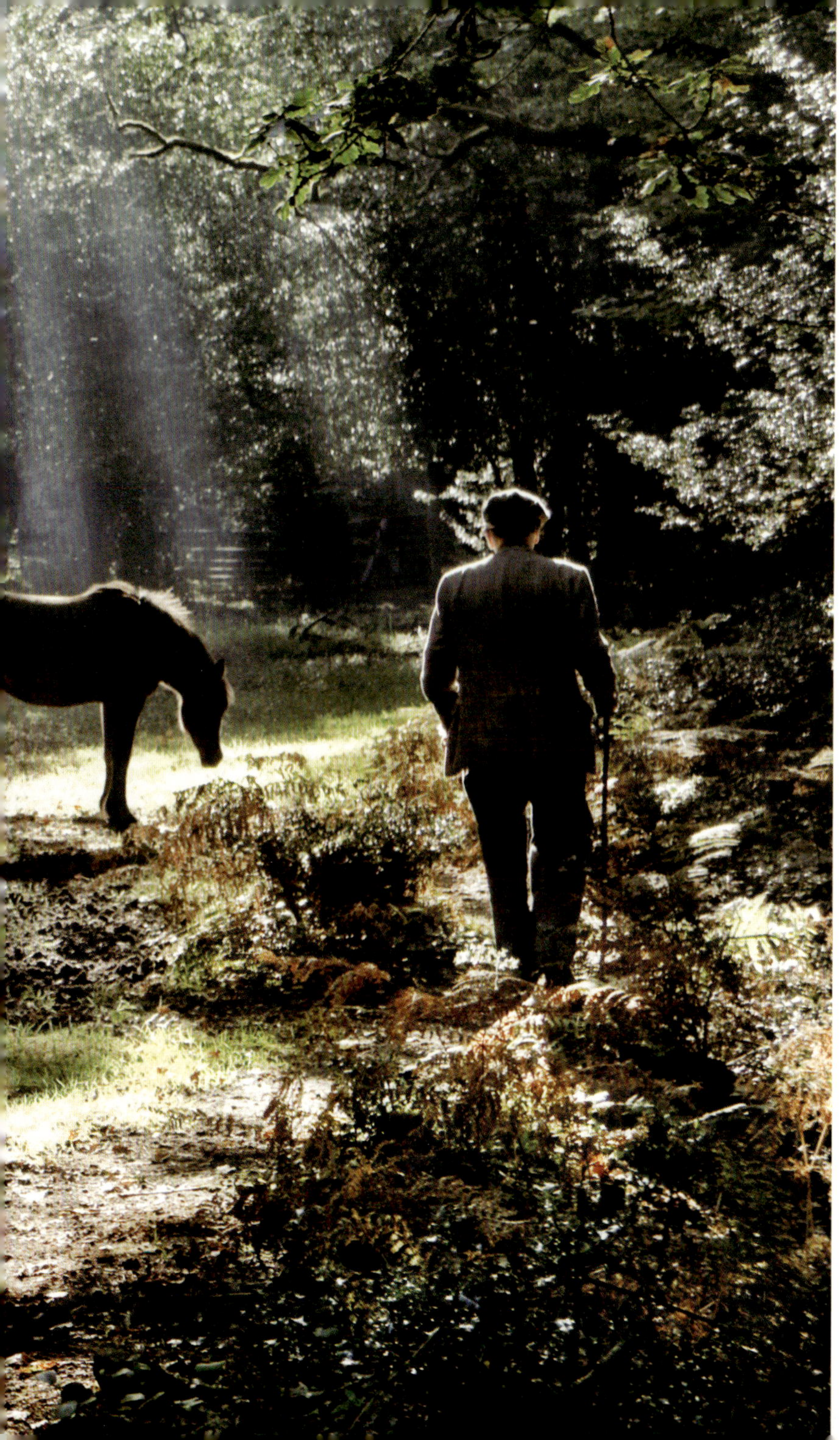

Introduction

It is almost impossible to truly understand the New Forest commoners' deep commitment to their environment. We can only admire it and support it to the best of our ability.

I first thought of publishing this book one sunny afternoon in November 2008. I met Agister Robert Maton shortly after he had humanely destroyed Eileen Gerrelli's beautiful filly foal, Lucky Lane Bunty II. Commoners Kelly Smith and her mother Christine Drodge had also stopped.

Kelly helped Robert catch Bunty who was wild and in pain from a badly smashed hind leg. She held the foal while Robert was forced to put her out of her misery. The Kennels came to load the dead foal on their vehicle. Bunty's mother Lucky Lane Kathleen watched.

The driver, who apparently wasn't speeding, clearly wasn't concentrating either. Visibility was good and there was no undergrowth nearby. Bunty had crossed the road to feed from her mother. She was a big strong filly that Eileen had decided to keep on the Forest rather than sell.

The browsing and grazing of the commoners' animals play a central part in the ecology of the New Forest. Without animals the Forest would also be a much less attractive and interesting place for visitors. It is very depressing for commoners when careless drivers do not seem to respect or value how blessed the nation is to have the New Forest.

My family are new commoners. We run four ponies on the Forest and we are members of the New Forest Commoners' Defence Association. This book is to celebrate the Centenary of the NFCDA with new photographs, alongside some 'favourites' and some commoning history. It demonstrates the commoners' long-term commitment to their New Forest and to each other.

Sally Fear

Ron Drodge walking through the woods at East Boldre, 2008.

Commoners of the New Forest

The New Forest is a region of 90,000 acres (approximately the size of the Isle of Wight) with its own laws and customs, lying between the Southampton water and the River Avon, in Hampshire.

The Forest has existed for centuries, originally as a hunting ground and a source of timber for shipbuilding. The Forest is made up of heathland, lawns for grazing animals, enclosures and marshy bottoms, which together create a unique habitat for a wide range of wildlife. Commoners, the people who farm and live on the Forest and who hold commoning rights over it, have a unique way of life that has not changed for hundreds of years. One theory is that the rights predate the Forest and were simply codified and regulated over the centuries.

These ancient 'rights of common' have led to a form of farming called commoning. The browsing and grazing of the commoners' animals has created a landscape that is rich in rare and unusual wildlife habitats and has led to the animals being called the 'architects of the forest'. The exercise of common rights is probably the only efficient and cost-effective way of managing such a large area of lowland heath. Just as the common rights are of ancient origin, so many of the methods of livestock management have remained largely unaltered over the centuries.

People born into commoning are proud of their long family histories. They are fiercely protective of the traditions in which they were brought up and are determined to see them survive. Until very recently, the practising commoners were almost exclusively members of the old Forest agricultural families. Today some residents who have moved into the area have become interested in the value of the custom and have begun to run a few animals on the Forest. Although they are welcome, they lack the

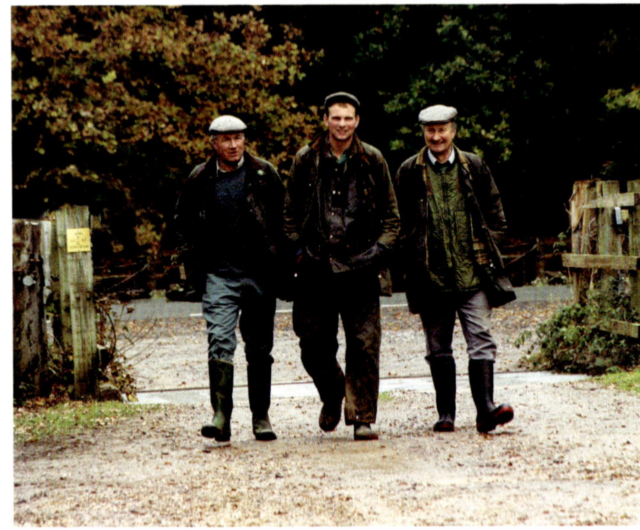

Above (left to right) John Stride, Robert Stride and his father Richard Stride at the end of a long hard drift in pouring rain, 2003. The Stride family have been commoning for generations, and their records to back to the 13th century. *Opposite* The Adams family ready for the Weirs drift (left to right) Nick, Mark, Cecil, John, Mervyn and Trevor, 2007.

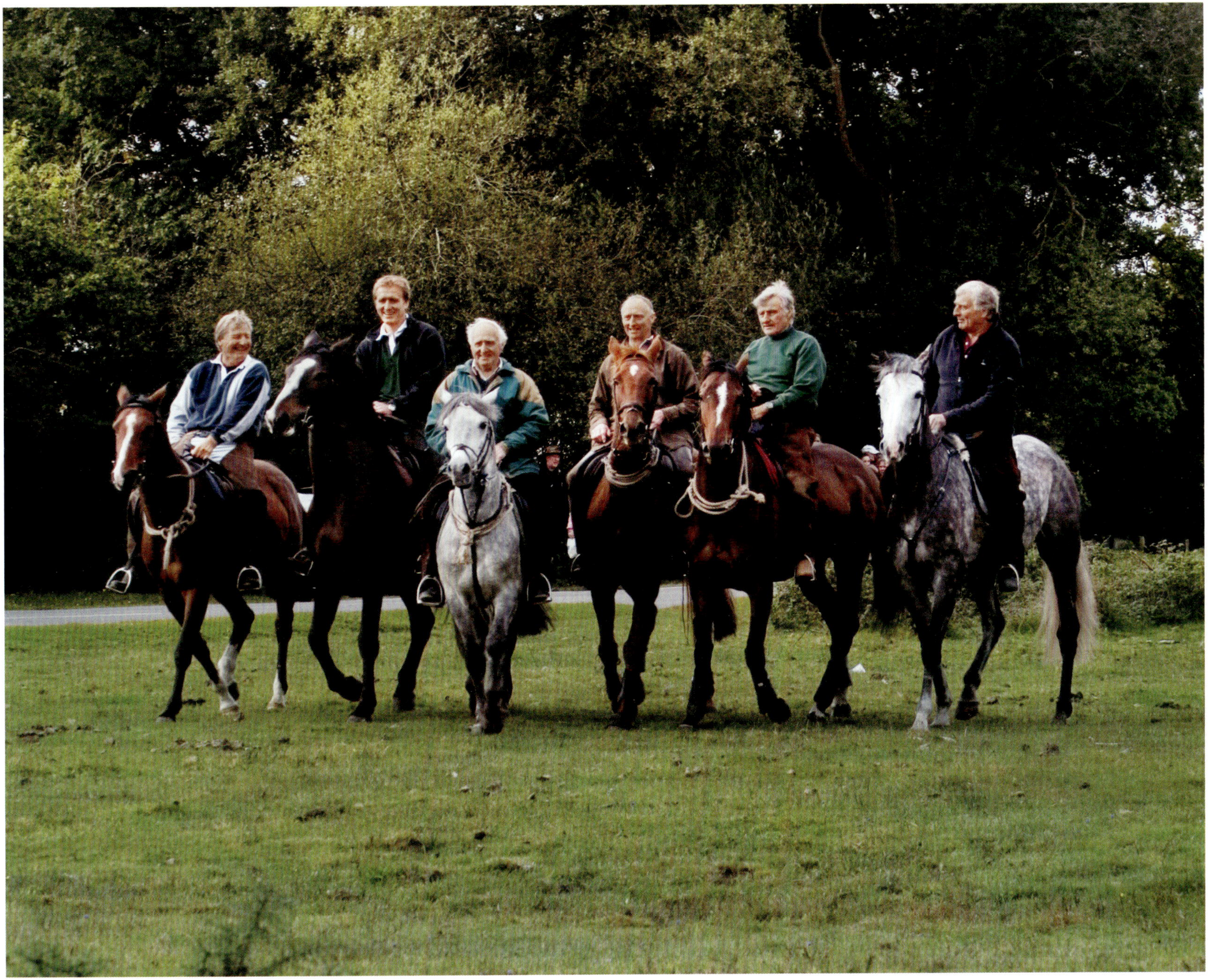

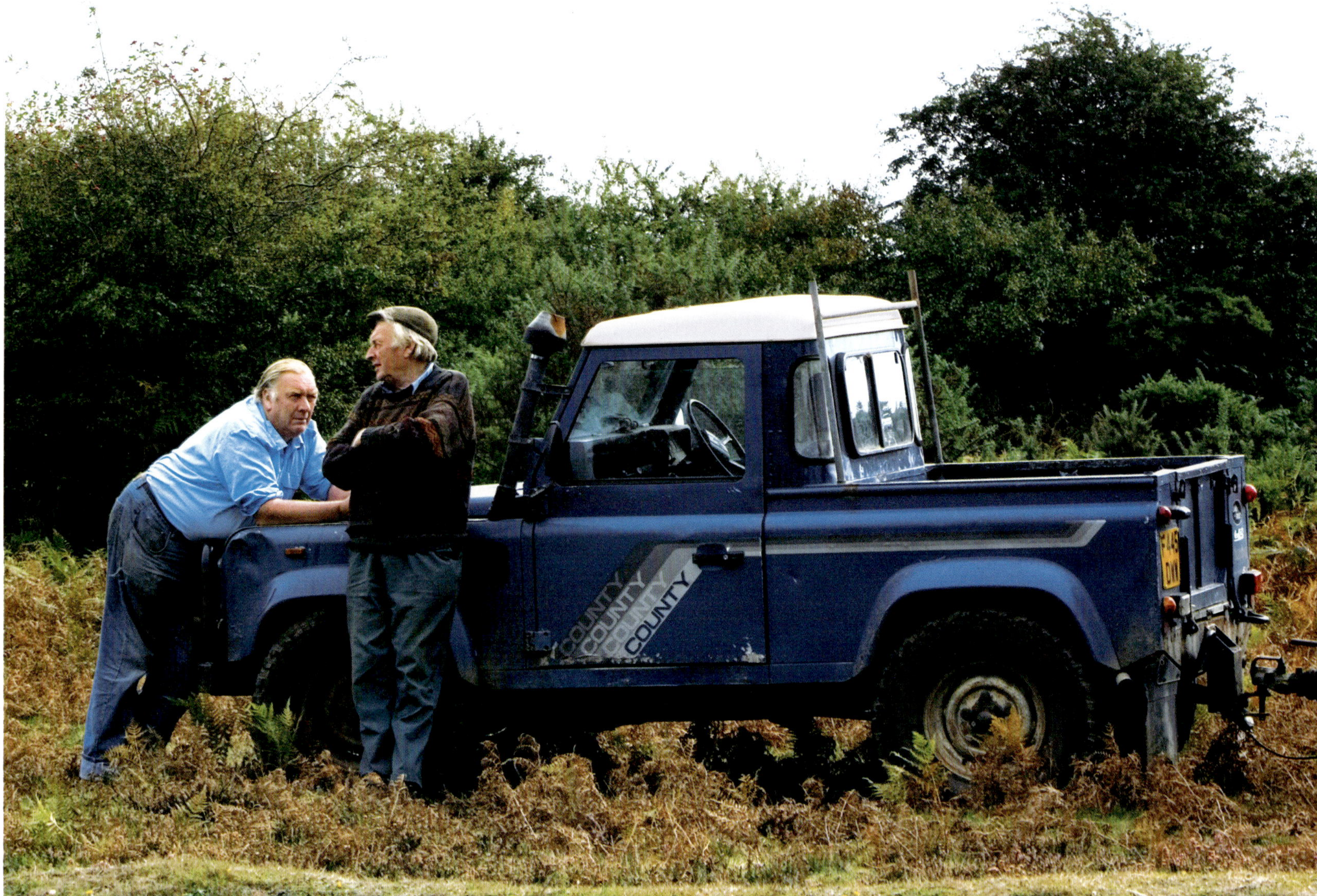
COUNTY
COUNTY
COUNTY
COUNTY

knowledge and skills that underpin the unique complex agricultural system and often regard their animals as pets.

Today there are approximately 600 practising commoners who are responsible for around 7,500 animals (mainly ponies) on the Forest. Exercising common rights is no longer profitable and the old commoning families run stock on the Forest because it is a tradition and because they love the way of life. 10% of the families own 80% of the stock and if they were to drift from commoning, there would not be many animals left on the Forest.

The commoners' interests are protected by the Verderers' Court, a body made up of five elected and five appointed officials. They look after the commoners' rights and work to preserve the natural beauty and traditional character of the Forest. The Verderers employ Agisters to look after the animals on the forest. Despite their crucial contribution to the maintenance of the Forest, commoners often feel misunderstood and undervalued. They are harassed by the increasing demands of those who use the Forest for recreation and their animals are often killed or injured by traffic in the Forest. The Commoners' Defence Association and the elected Verderers protect their interests but the greatest threat to this ancient way of life is the chronic shortage of affordable housing.

The dramatic increase in property prices – small-holdings often start at twice the price of an average house which has put ownership of land beyond the average commoner. Land that has belonged to commoning families for centuries is rapidly being lost. As a result, many young people now have to choose between living with their parents in order to continue with the way of life, or moving out of the area.

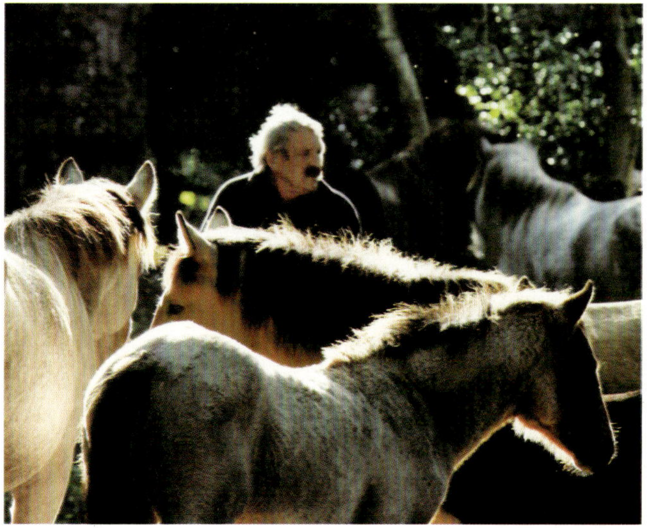

Opposite The Rickman brothers wait for their ponies to come in on the Latchmoor drift, 2005.
Above Kenny Drodge looking for his ponies after the East Boldre drift, 2008.

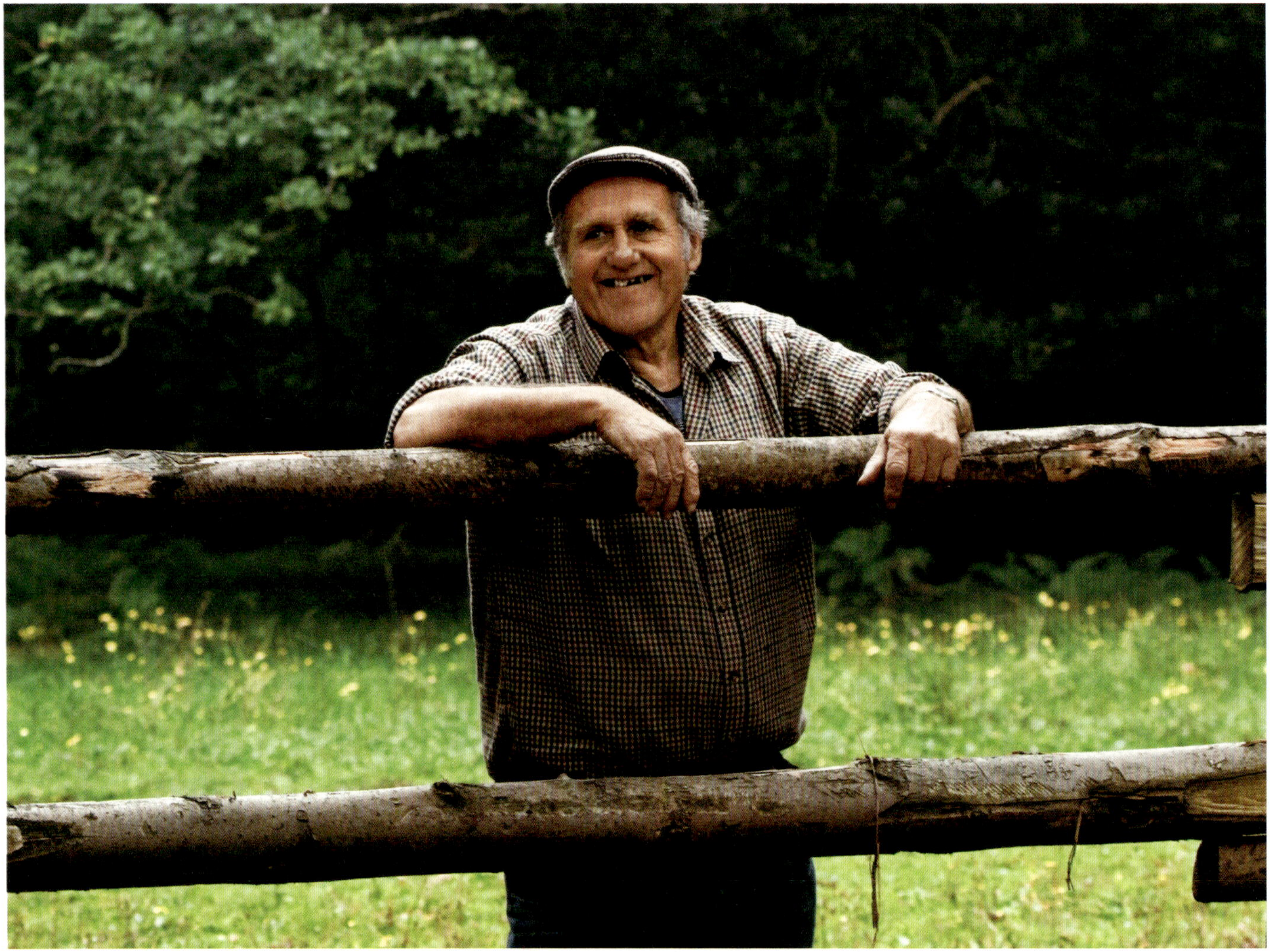

Above Derek Ingram after a successful day on the Ipley drift, 2008.
Opposite Len Mansbridge talking to his grandson Alan Ingram after the Holmsley drift, 2003. The family have been commoning for generations over three centuries.

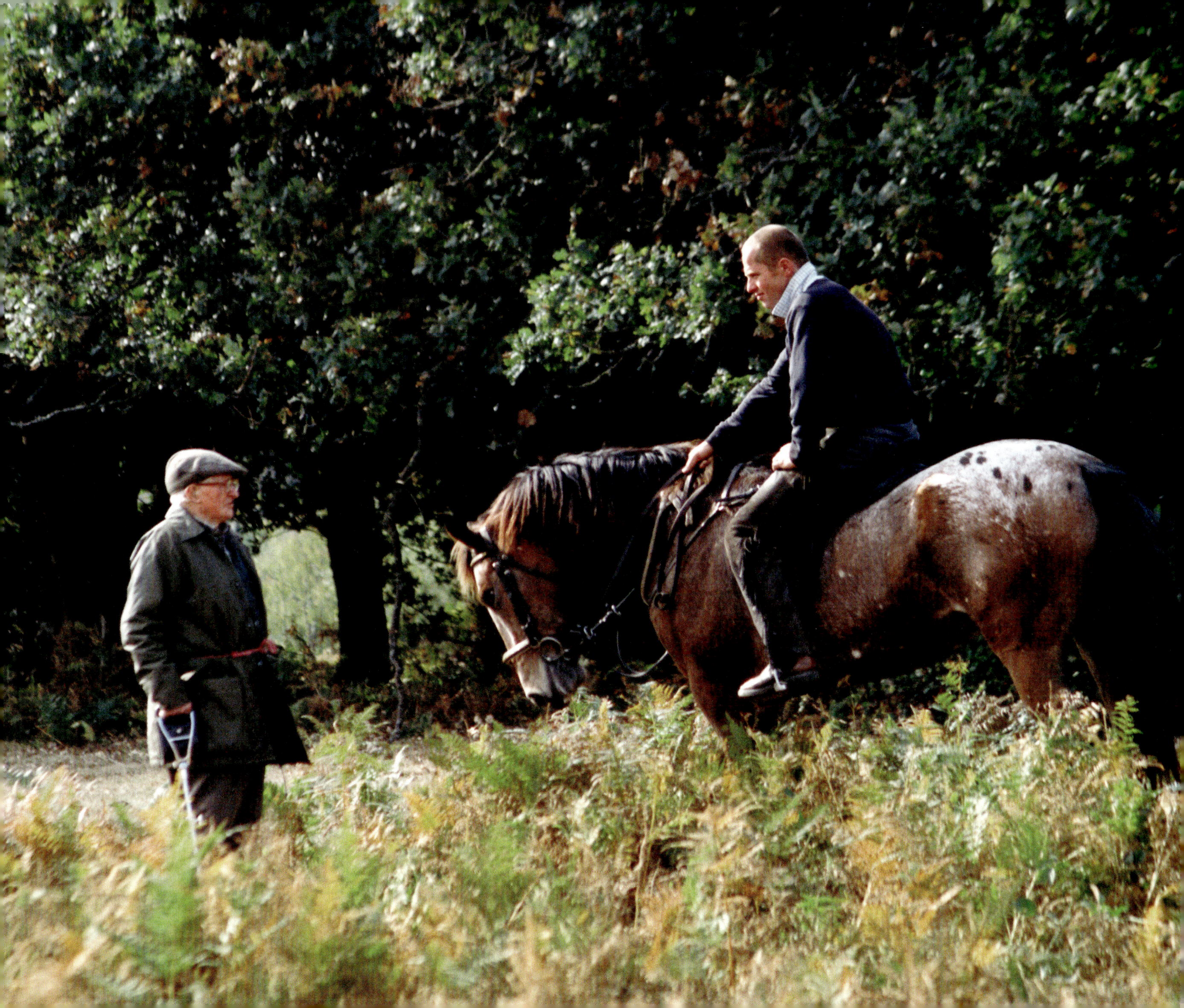

The Verderers

There are ten Verderers, five who are appointed and five who are elected. Their primary objective is to regulate and protect the commoners' interests and to preserve the natural beauty and traditional character of the Forest. By law, they are not permitted to profit from their office.

In order to qualify to be a Verderer a candidate must occupy, but not necessarily own, one acre of land to which rights of pasture over the New Forest are attached.

The Crown appoints the Official Verderer. The Department for Environment, Food and Rural Affairs, the Forestry Commission, the Countryside Agency and the Planning Authority are responsible for the other four appointed Verderers. They each serve for varying amounts of time. The five elected Verderers serve for a period of six years. They are elected by the commoners for their immense knowledge and unequivocal commitment to the New Forest. Between them they possess an extraordinary variety of skills and expertise. This is the great strength of the Court.

As the demands on the Forest have increased over the years, so too have the demands on the Verderers. In addition to an in-depth knowledge of the Forest, Forest law and animal husbandry, they now have to know about EU regulations and National Park law.

Anyone can attend the Verderers' Court. Any commoner or any member of the public wishing to make a statement or complaint in public on Forest matters, is permitted to make a 'presentment' to the Court.

The Verderers employ the Agisters.

Opening Words Of Court
Announced by Jonathan Gerrelli, Head Agister
Oyez, Oyez, Oyez! All manner of persons who have any presentment to make or matter or thing to do at this Court of Verderers, let them come forward and they shall be heard. God save the Queen.

Jonathan Gerrelli, Head Agister, opens the Verderers' Court 2006, watched by three other Agisters (left to right) Andrew Napthine, Robert Maton and Mike Lovell. The fifth Agister, Peter Rix, was on an emergency call out.

The Verderers back row (left to right): Patricia Thorne (appointed by DEFRA), Kathy Heron (appointed by HCC), Dionis Macnair (elected), Oliver Crosthwaite Eyre (Official Verderer appointed by the Crown), The Hon Ralph Montagu (appointed by the Forestry Commission), Anthony Pasmore (elected), Anthony Gerrelli (elected), John Adams (elected) and Peter Frost (appointed by the Countryside Agency). Jeffrey Kitcher (elected) was unavailable.

Front row (left to right): Susan Westwood (Clerk to the Verderers), Mike Seddon (Forestry Commission Deputy Surveyor) and Will Parke (Forestry Commission Area Land Agent).

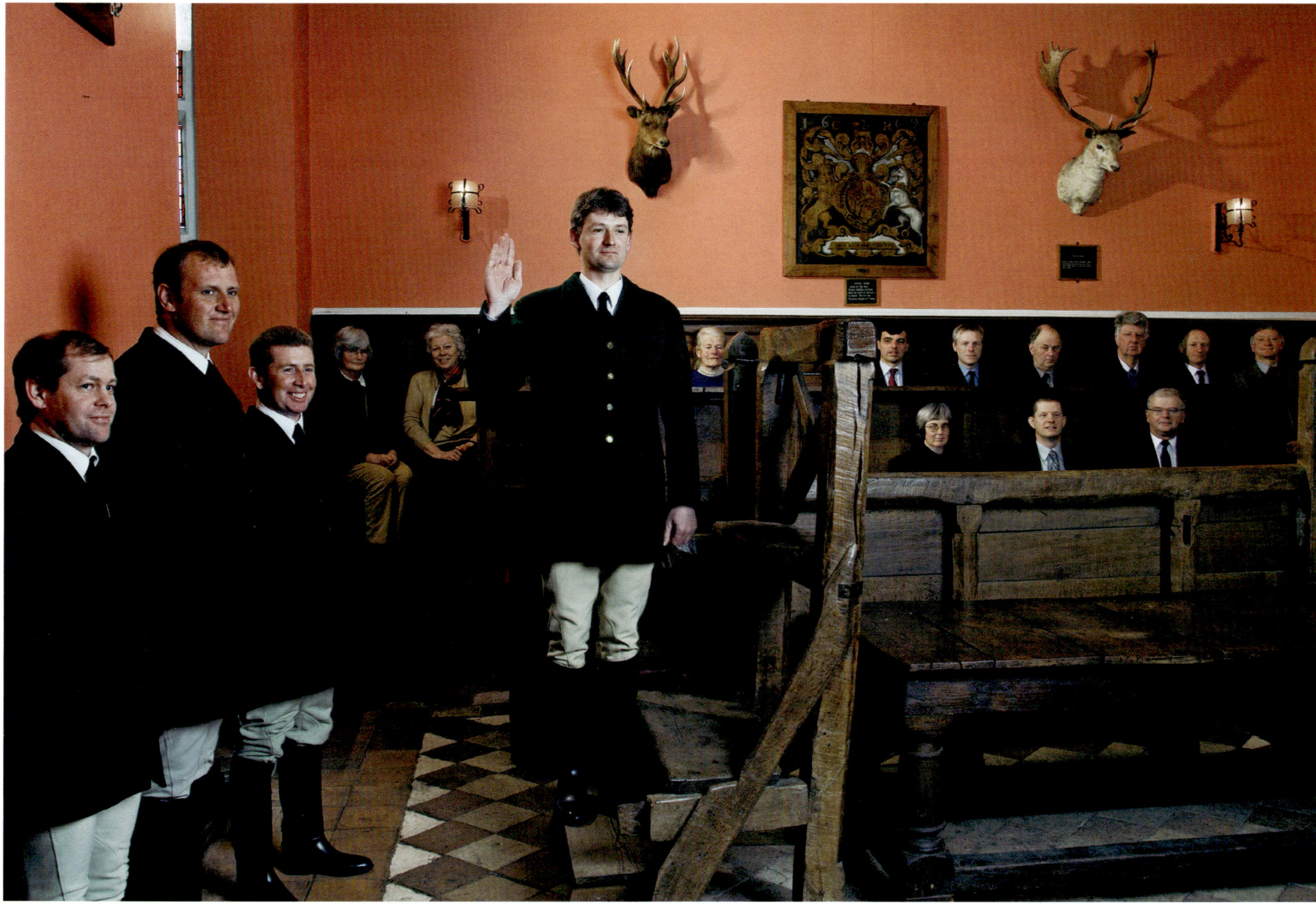

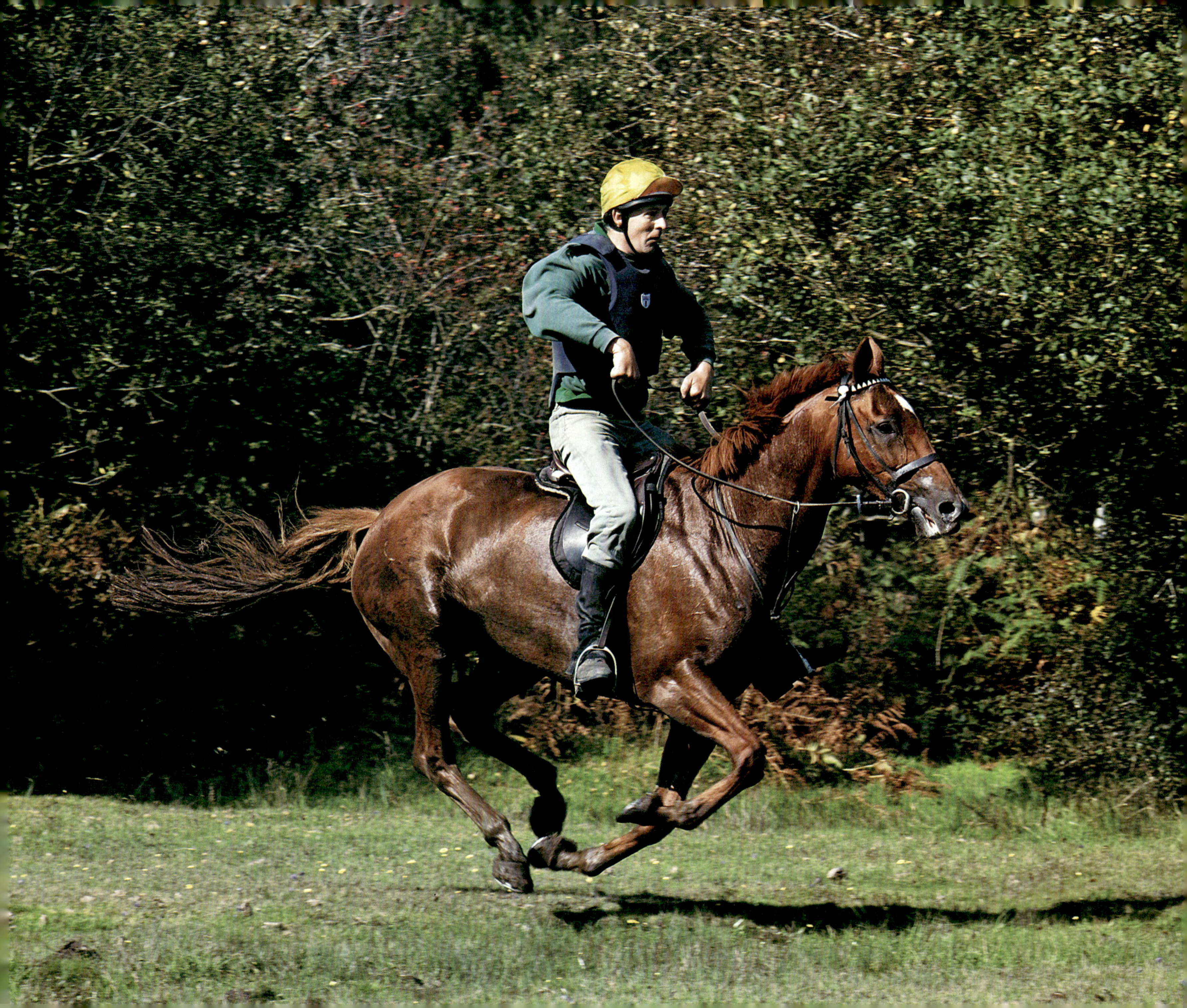

The Agisters

There are five Agisters, one Head Agister and four colleagues. They are on call 24 hours a day, seven days a week. They are all commoners with an intimate knowledge of the Forest. Each Agister must be adept at handling all types of livestock, be an excellent rider and able to work on his own and as part of a team in the rough Forest conditions The Agisters are ambassadors for the Forest and dealing with the public is a large part of their job.

As one commoner said as she watched two Agisters handling a wild colt: "Our Agisters are real men, they didn't get their muscles in the gym, they got them on the Forest!"

Agisters go out in all weathers responding to calls regarding problems with any of the animals. They know all the animals in their area well, often recognising them from a great distance. They know to whom each animal belongs and their general condition. If an animal is ill, in poor condition or a danger to other animals, the Agisters have the right to order it off the forest.

The Agisters collect the 'marking fees', the payment a commoner makes for each animal he or she runs on the Forest. This goes towards paying their salaries.

In the late summer and early autumn the Agisters arrange the drifts (or round ups) of the commoners' ponies.

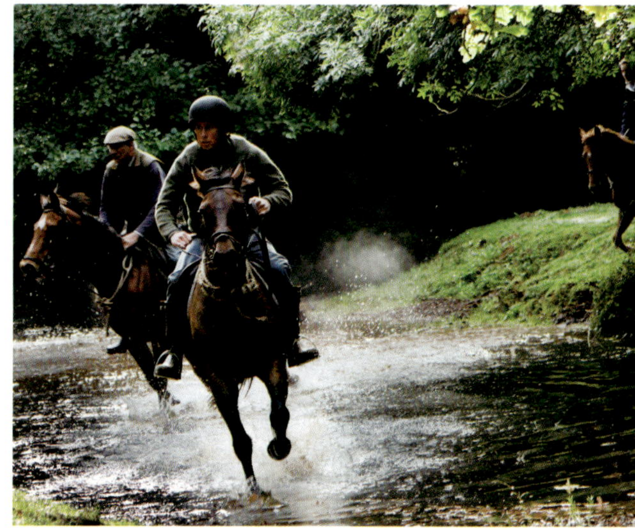

Opposite Jonathan Gerrelli, Head Agister, gallops fast to head off the ponies before they reach the road. Weirs drift 2008.
Above Agister Mike Lovell leading commoners John and Beth Stride over the water at New Park, 2005.

Stock on the Forest

The numbers of depastured animals on the Forest varies from year to year. In 2008 there were approximately 4,500 ponies, 2,500 cattle, 125 donkeys and 440 pigs. The amount of stock on the Forest can vary from week to week.

The New Forest pony is much more than a tourist attraction. It is essential for the survival of this ancient pastured woodland. The ponies don't just graze, they also browse, eating and enjoying the nutritional gorse, holly, ivy and brambles. They grow thick, bristly moustaches to protect their muzzles. In winter, their thick coats provide them with warmth and the dense bushes provide excellent shelter from wind and driving rain.

The Verderers' Stallion Scheme has improved the stock of ponies on the Forest. The scheme selects the finest stallions, usually around 40, but the number is reviewed every year, and the amount of time they stay on the Forest is restricted. The stallion inspections take place once a year and generally any mature stallion that is not selected is kept in the owner's fields. The younger colts (stallions) are castrated to be riding ponies. Commoners can also apply for their mares to be graded. They are judged on conformation, movement and type. This ensures that the quality of foals now being born on the Forest has improved and the sale prices have increased.

Some stallions can be difficult to keep in a domestic environment. During the winter months grazing is made available specifically for the Forest run stallions in New Park, Brockenhurst and on the Cadland Estate at Fawley. Approximately 20 Forest stallions are put in one large field together and after a bit of an exciting kick off, they quickly settle down demonstrating their special temperament.

Some commoners run cattle on the Forest and these have to be freeze branded or ear tagged with their owner's brand. Various types of cattle dwell on the Forest, including Belted Galloways, Dexters, Charolais, Herefords, Simmental and Belgian Blue. The most distinctive are the Highland cattle. Cattle can be kept out all year but usually come back at night during the winter when there is not much to eat. Some cattle are just turned out in the summer which they love. Their happiness and the Forest grazing seems to add to the quality of their meat.

Donkeys fetch good prices at the sales but they are vulnerable as they are more likely to be fed by the roadside or stolen.

Pigs are allowed onto the Forest during the autumn pannage season, which lasts for around sixty days. The pigs eat the fallen acorns which can be poisonous to ponies and cattle. Some sows which are in pig (expecting piglets) are allowed on the Crown land after the pannage season, but the owners must first obtain written permission from the Forestry Commission. These pigs are known as Privilege Sows. There is a delicious and very distinctive taste to pork that has fed on Forest acorns.

Two-year old colts are inspected by the New Forest Pony Breeding and Cattle Society for their stallion licence. John Adams shows his Burley Timelord who passed, 2009.

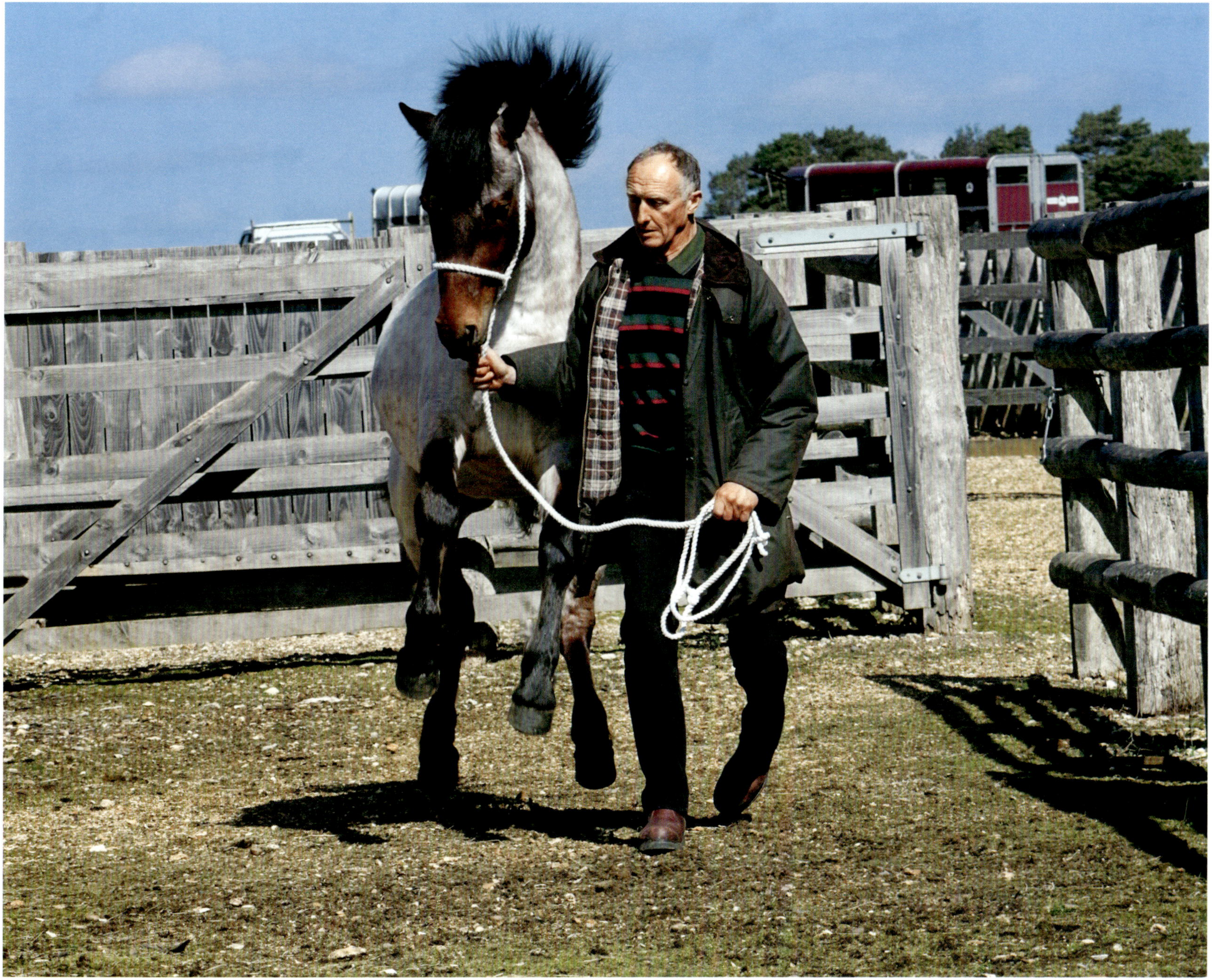

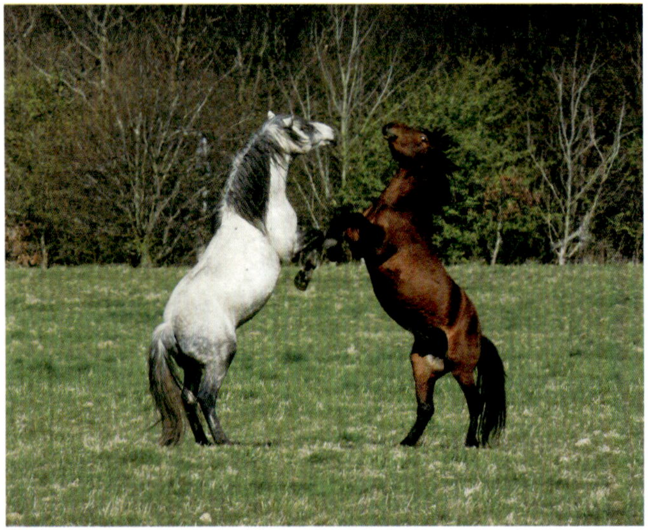

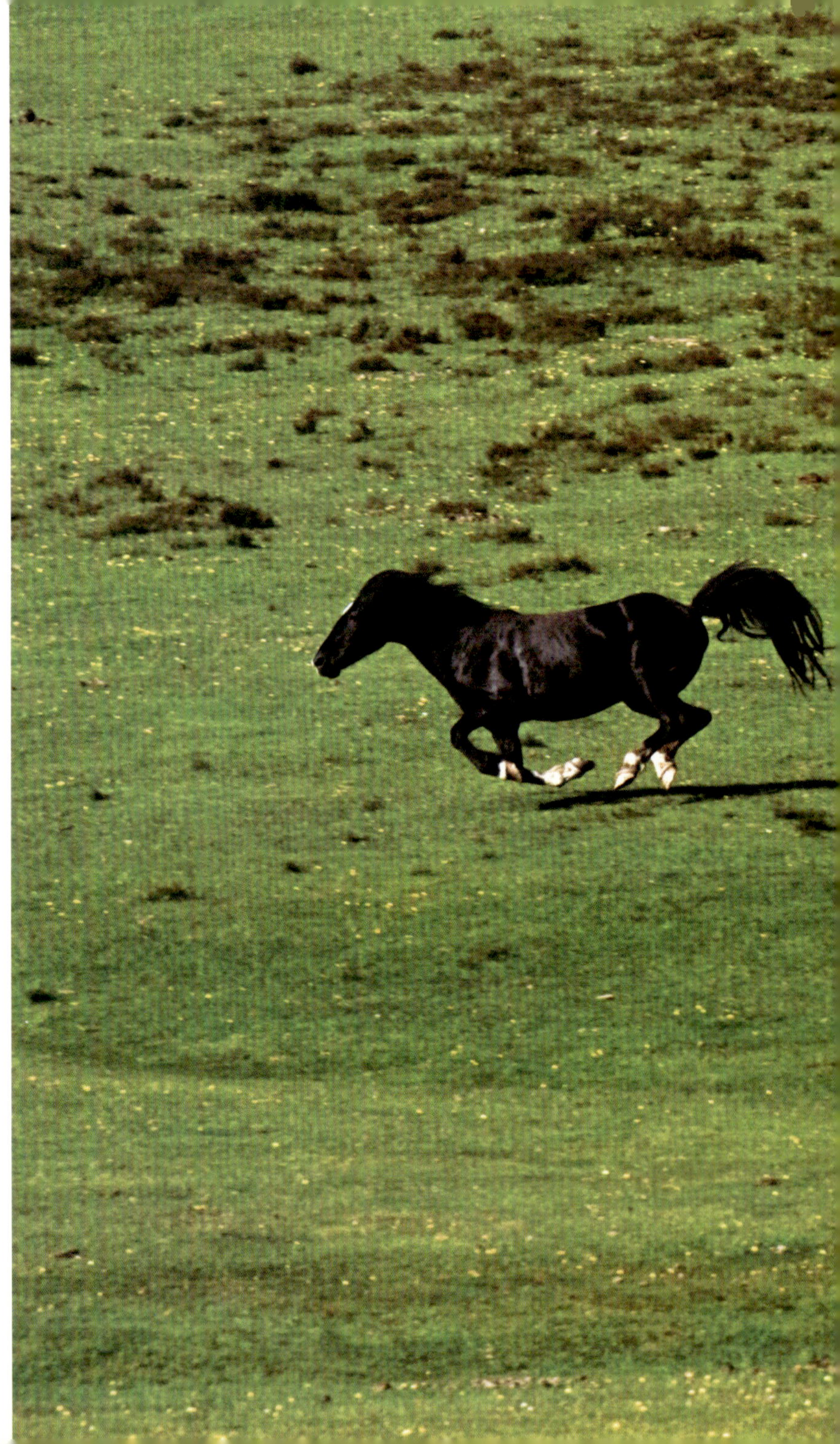

Above Stallions Furzey Lodge Zennica (left) and Lovelyhill High Exchange (right) playing on the winter grazing. Cadland Estate, 2009.
Opposite Stallion Brookshill Royal chasing a mare across Longslade, 2008.

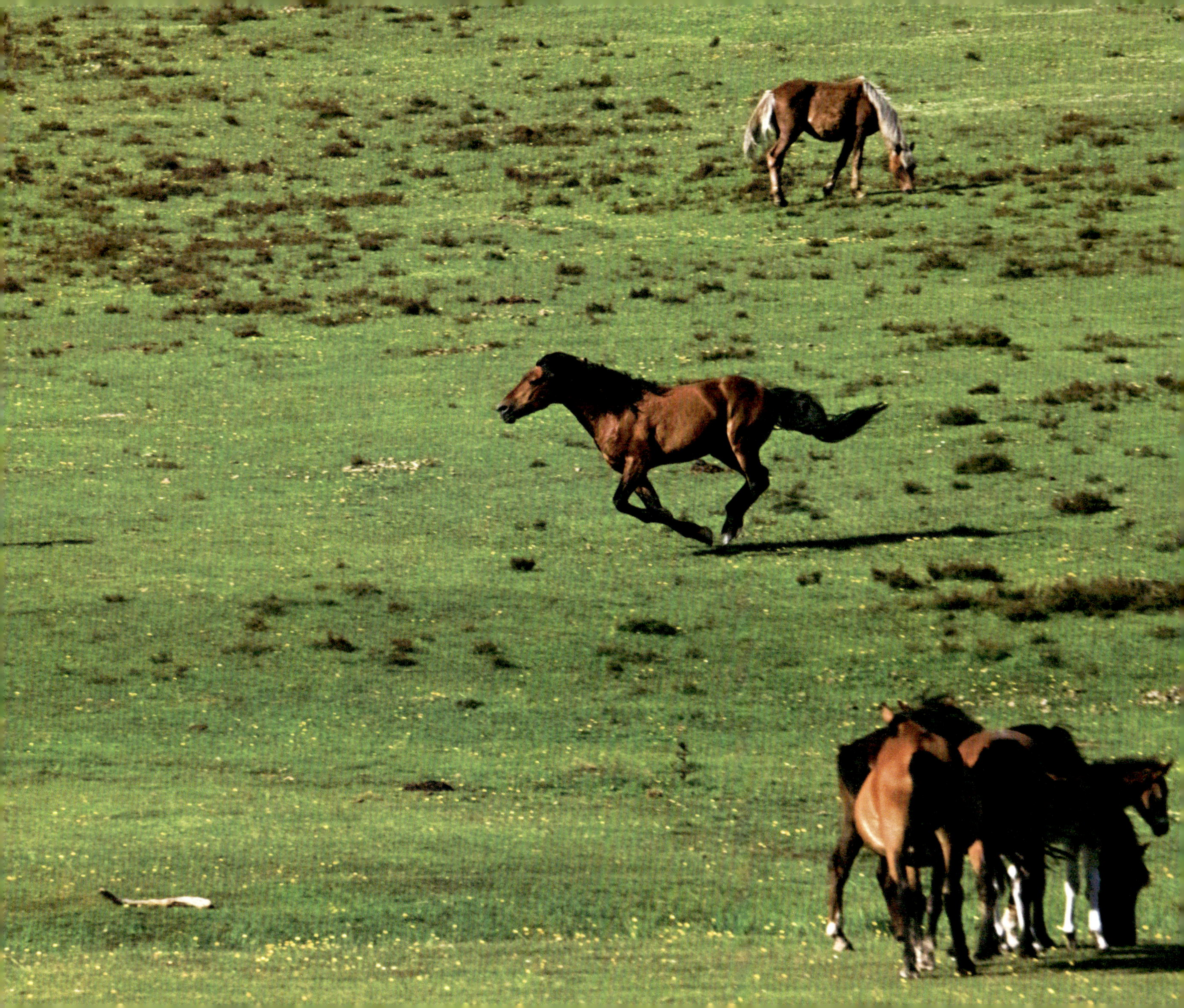

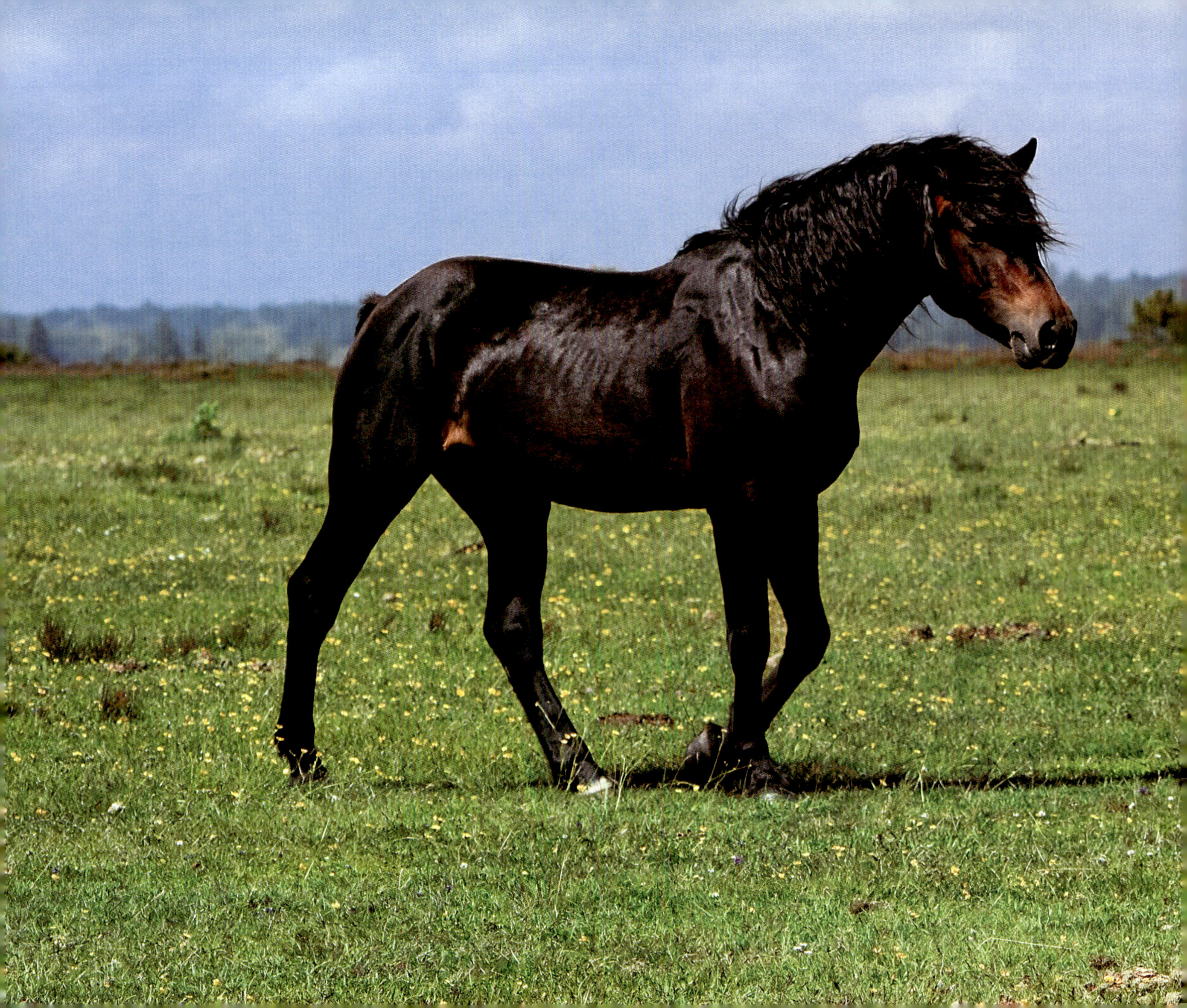

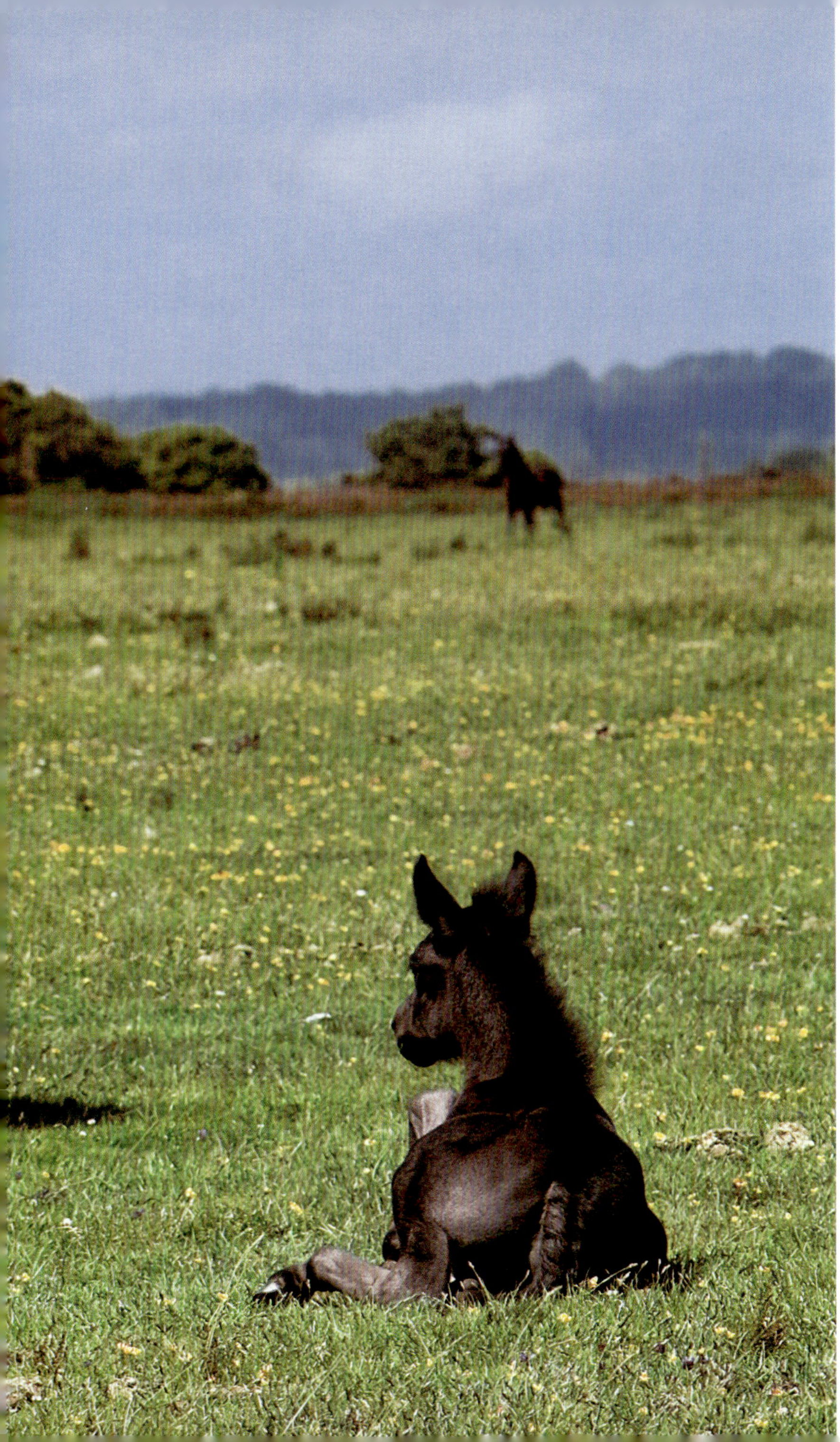

Stallion Brookshill Mustang greets one of his offspring on Wilverley, 2008.

The New Forest is an area of international importance. It is Britain's richest 'Nature Reserve'.
Colin Tubbs

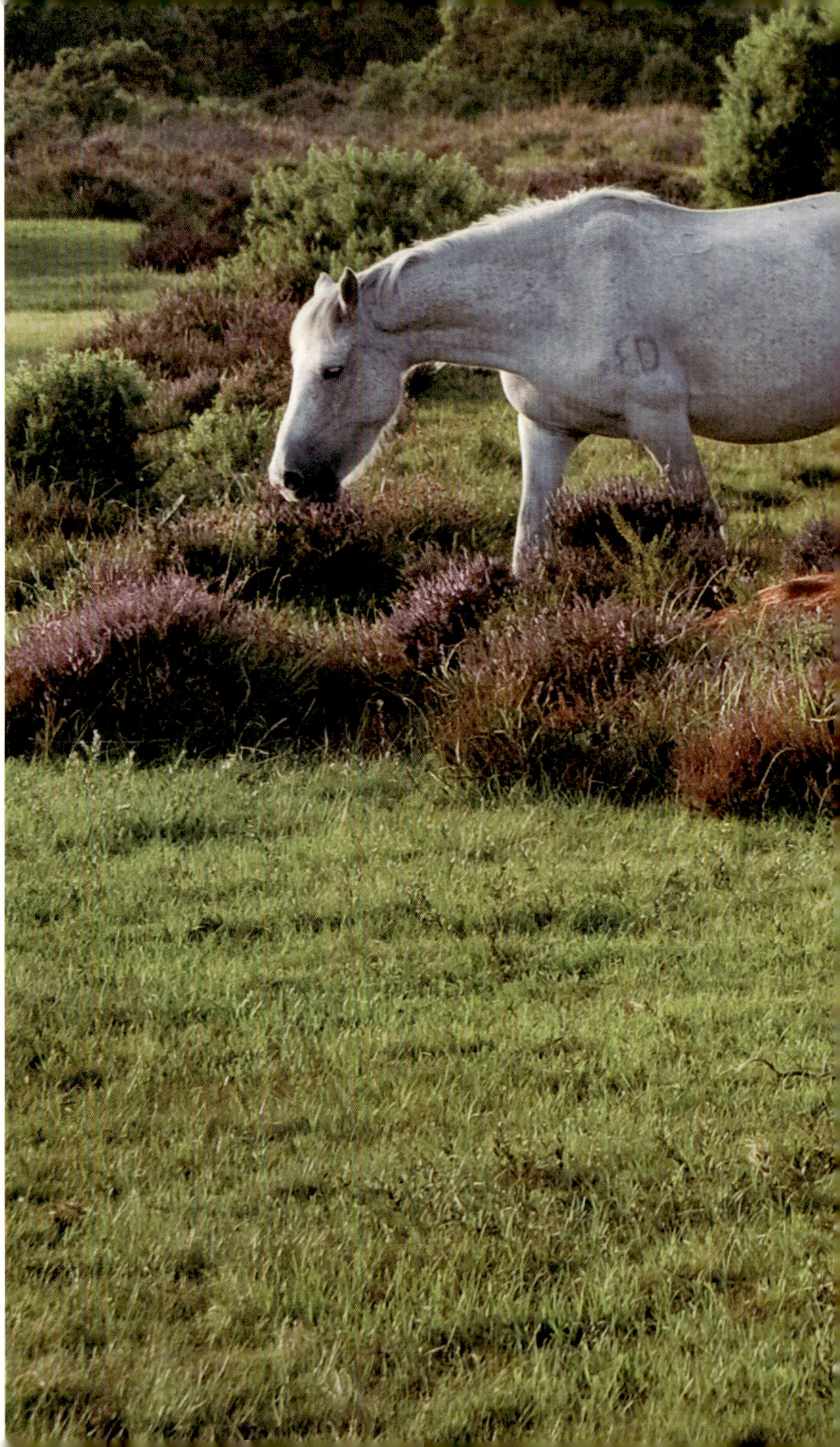

Mark Adams' mare and foal wander through cattle belonging to John Weiler on Setley, 2006.

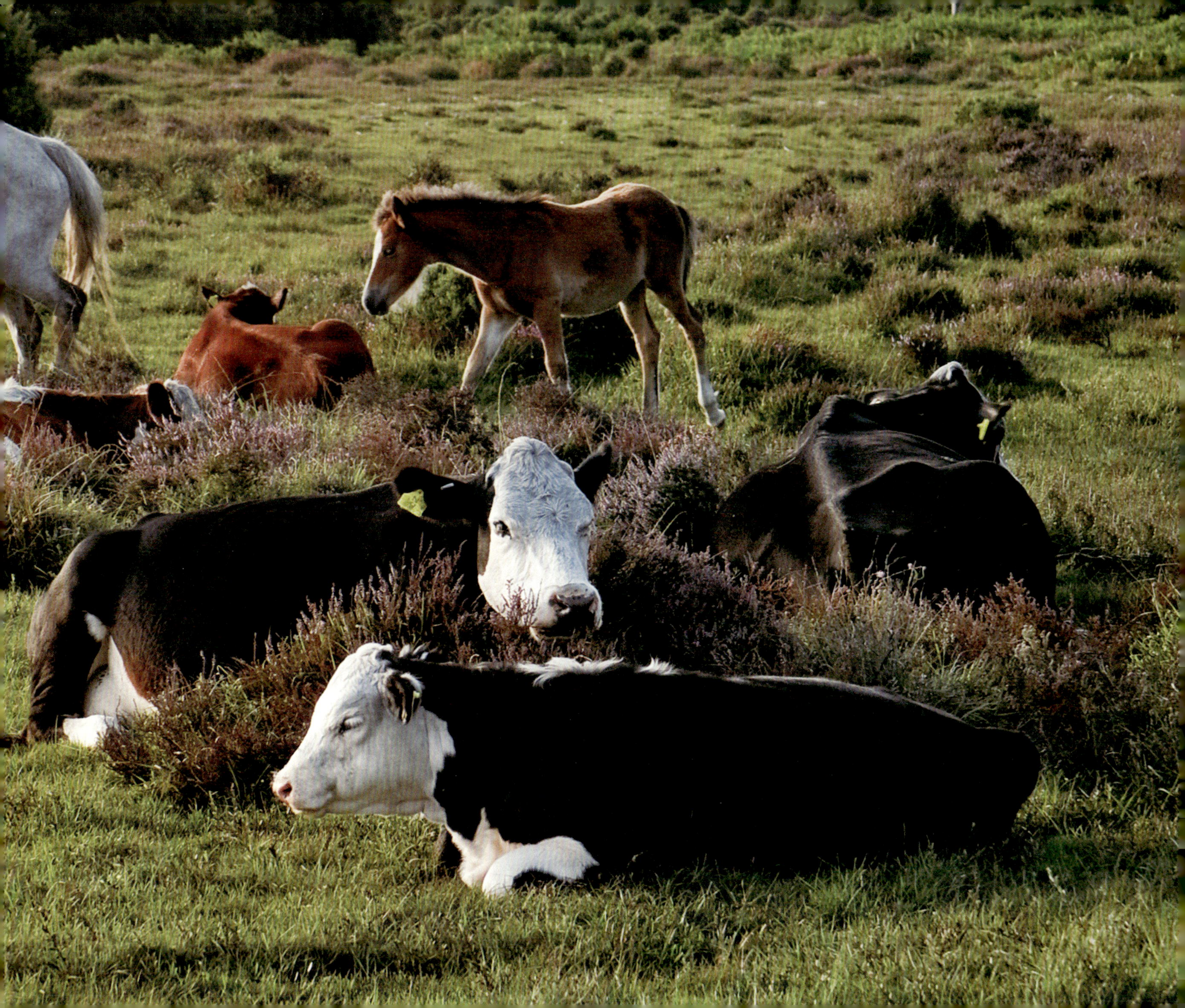

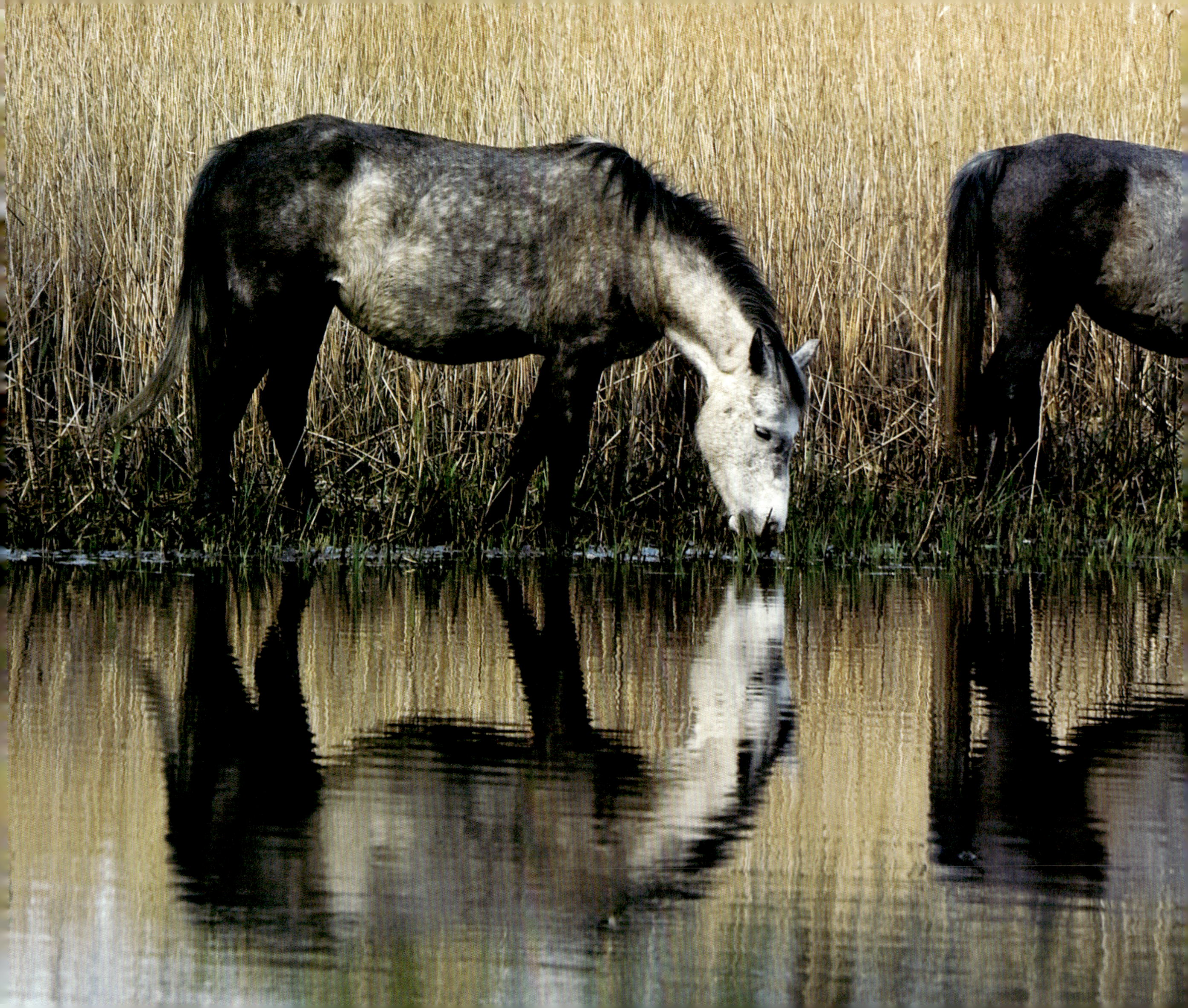

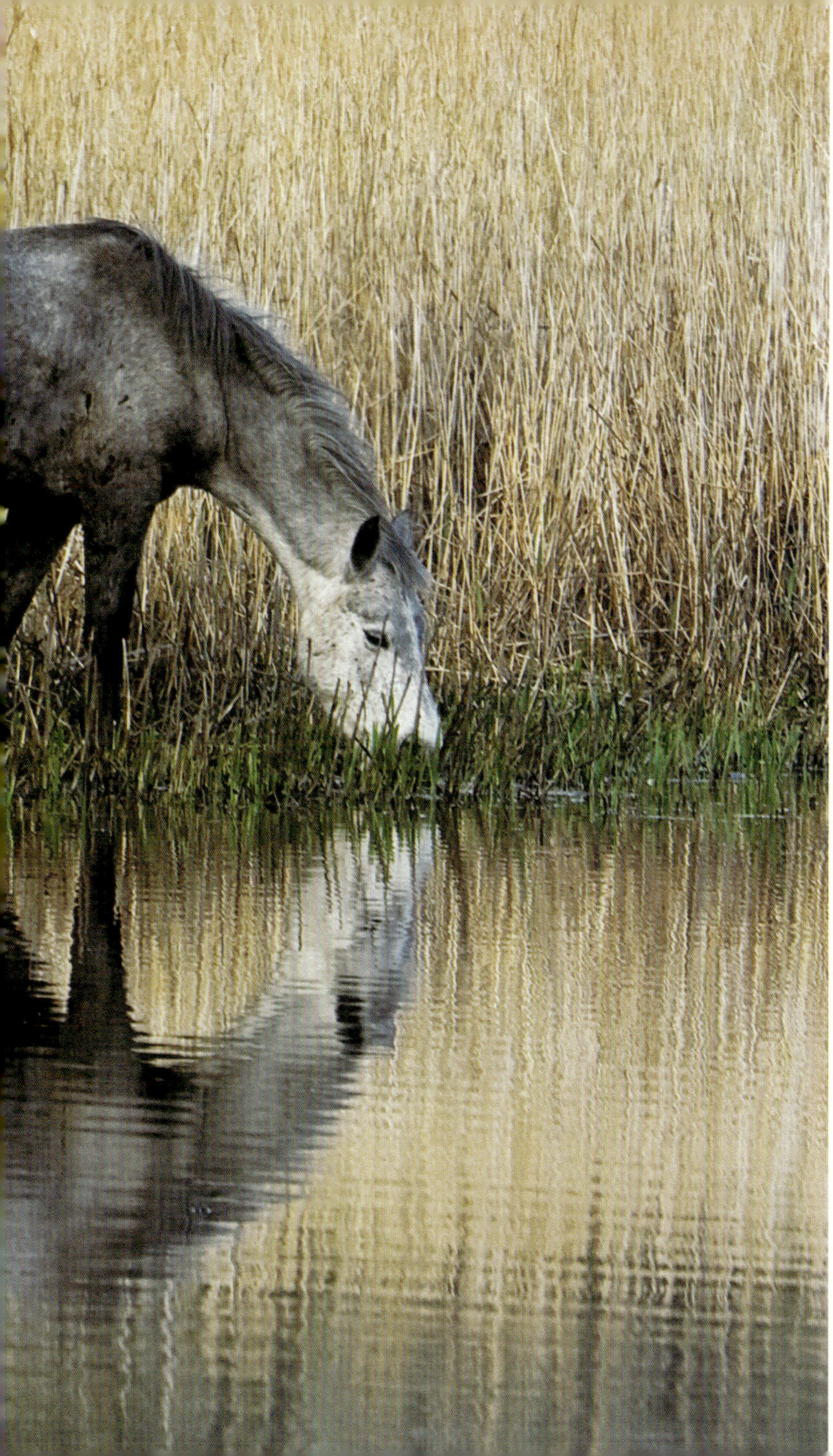

10% of the commoning families own 80% of the stock, so if these families ever drift from commoning, there won't be many animals left on the Forest.

Ray Readhead's New Forest mares grazing at Beaulieu, 2007.

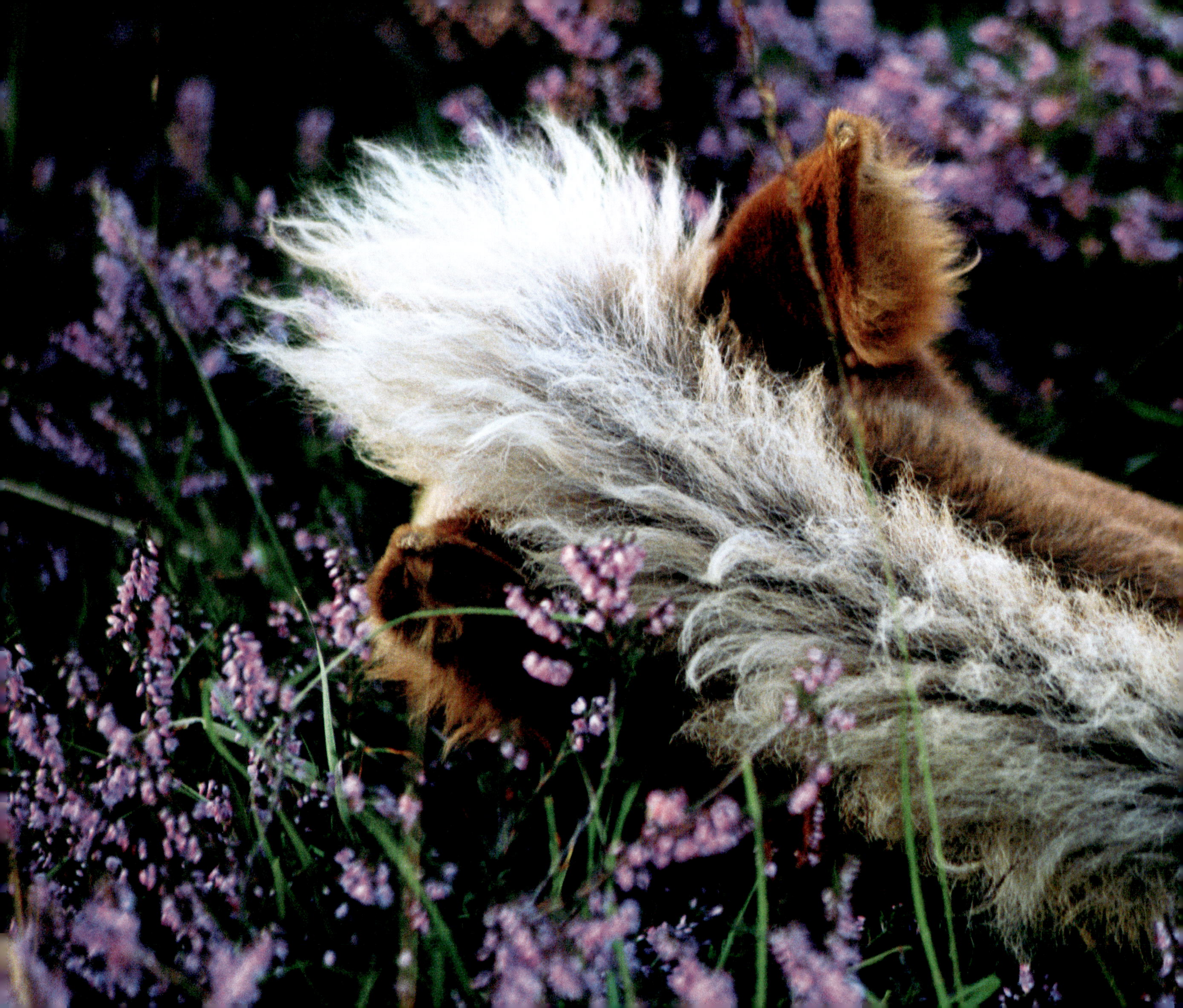

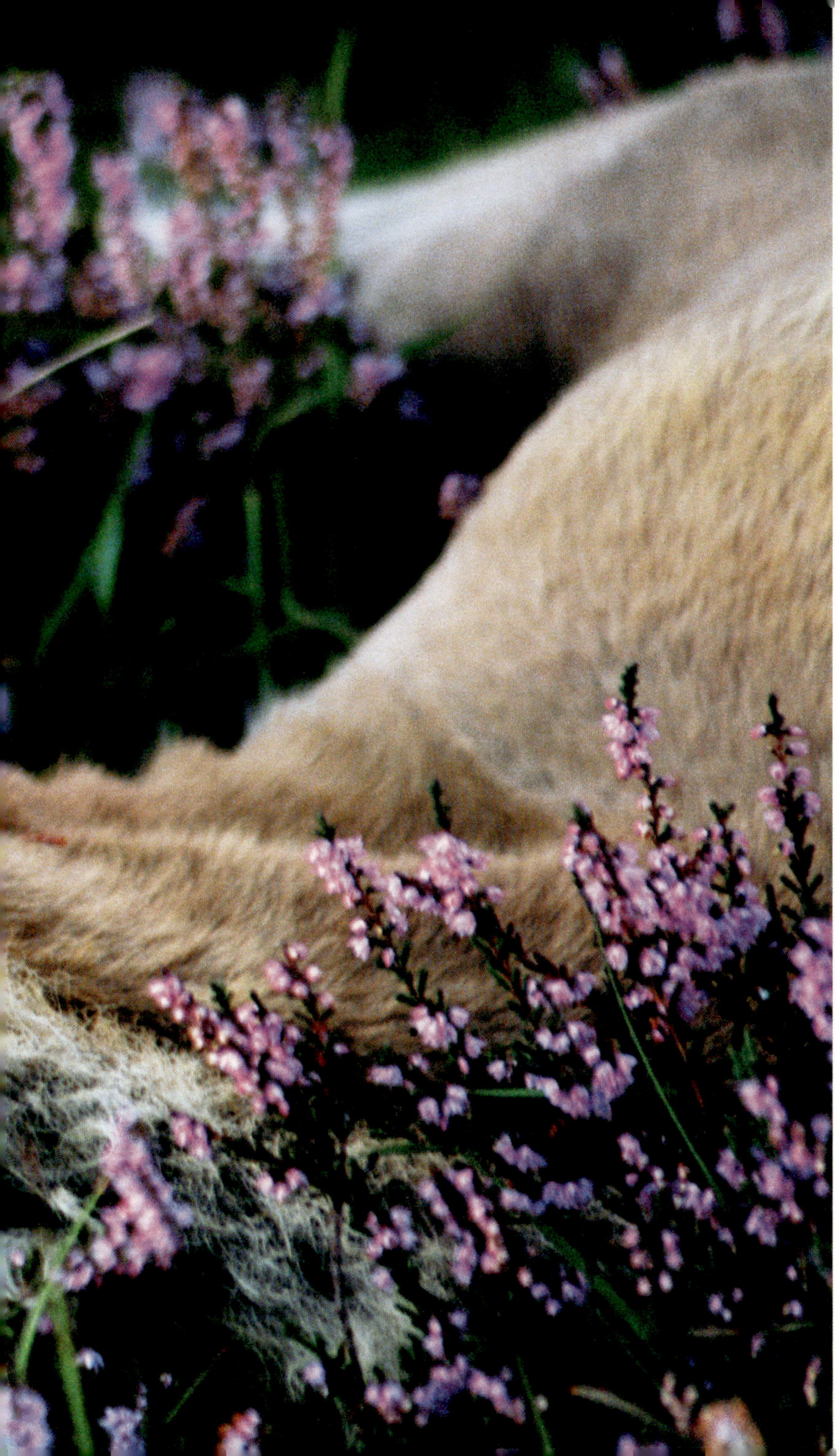

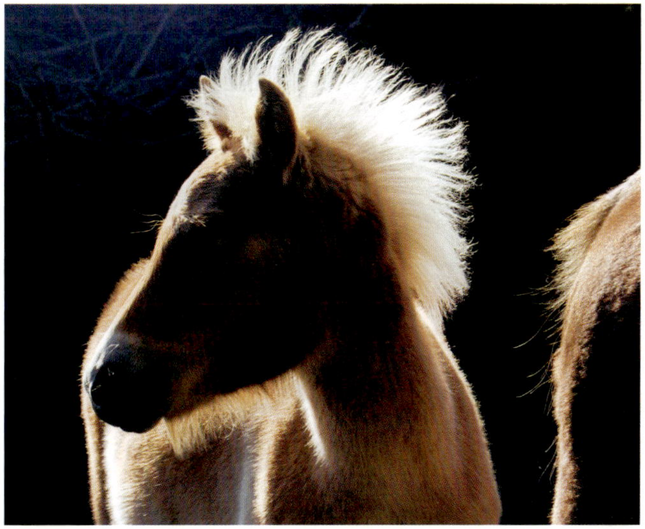

Opposite New Forest foal asleep in the heather on Beaulieu Heath, 2003.
Above Foal that has recently come in on the Fritham drift, 2005.
Following left The eye of Mary's Midnight, New Forest mare, 2004.
Following right The eyes of New Forest mares, recently come in on drifts, 2005.

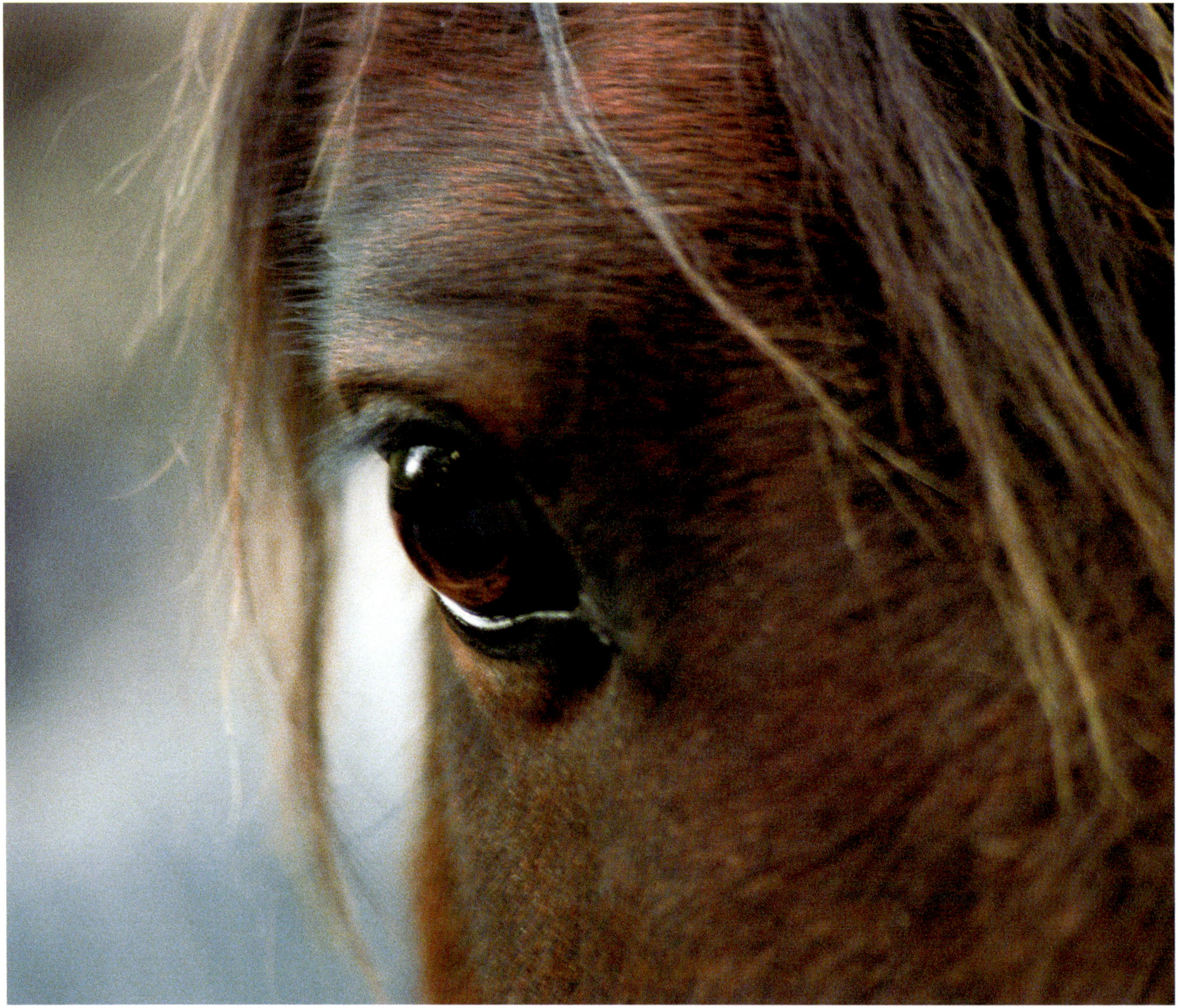

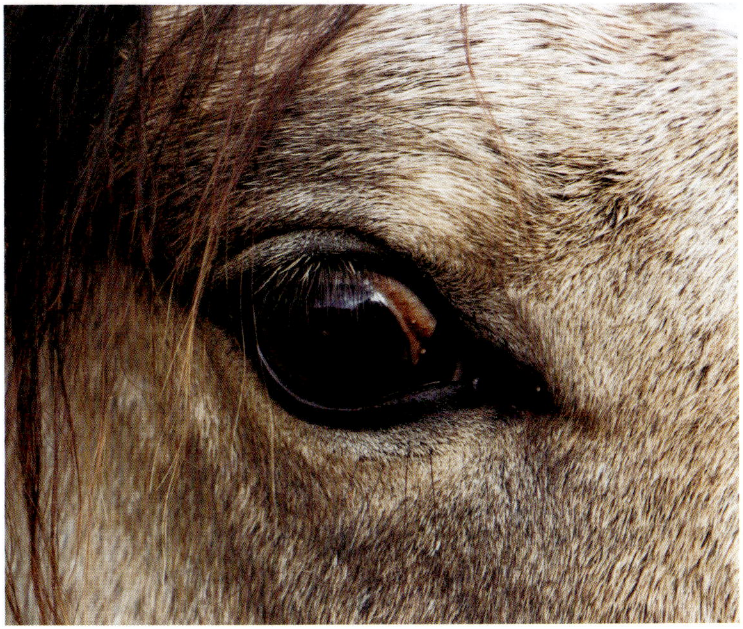
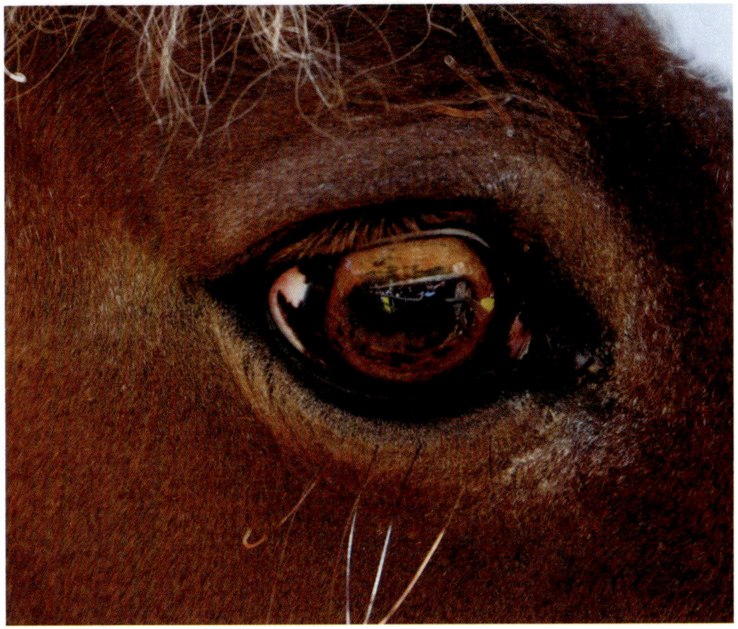
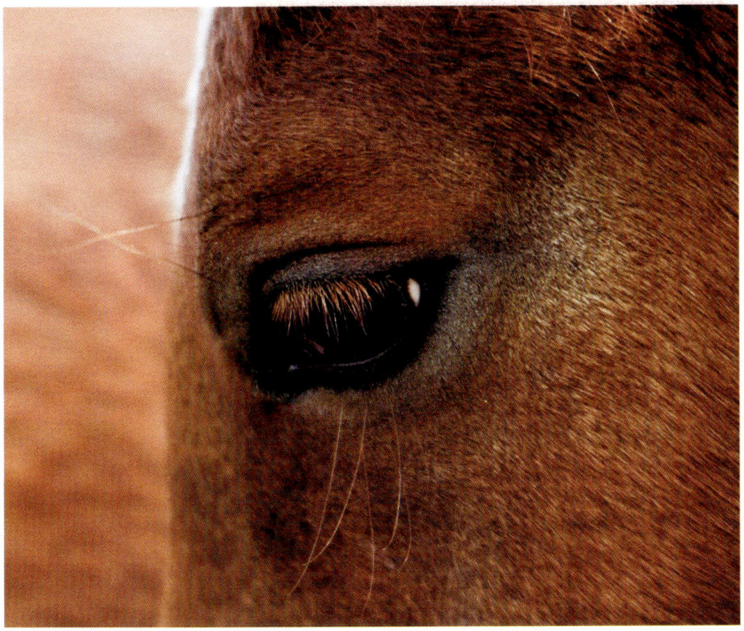
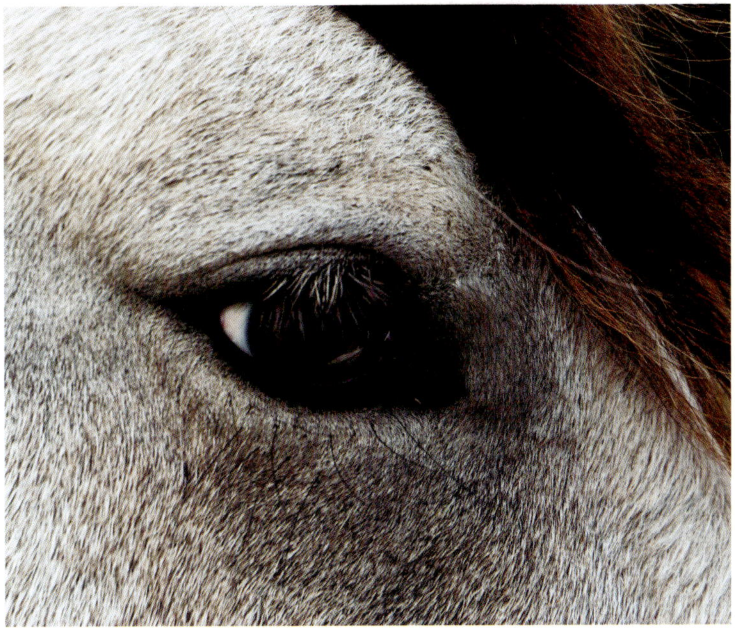

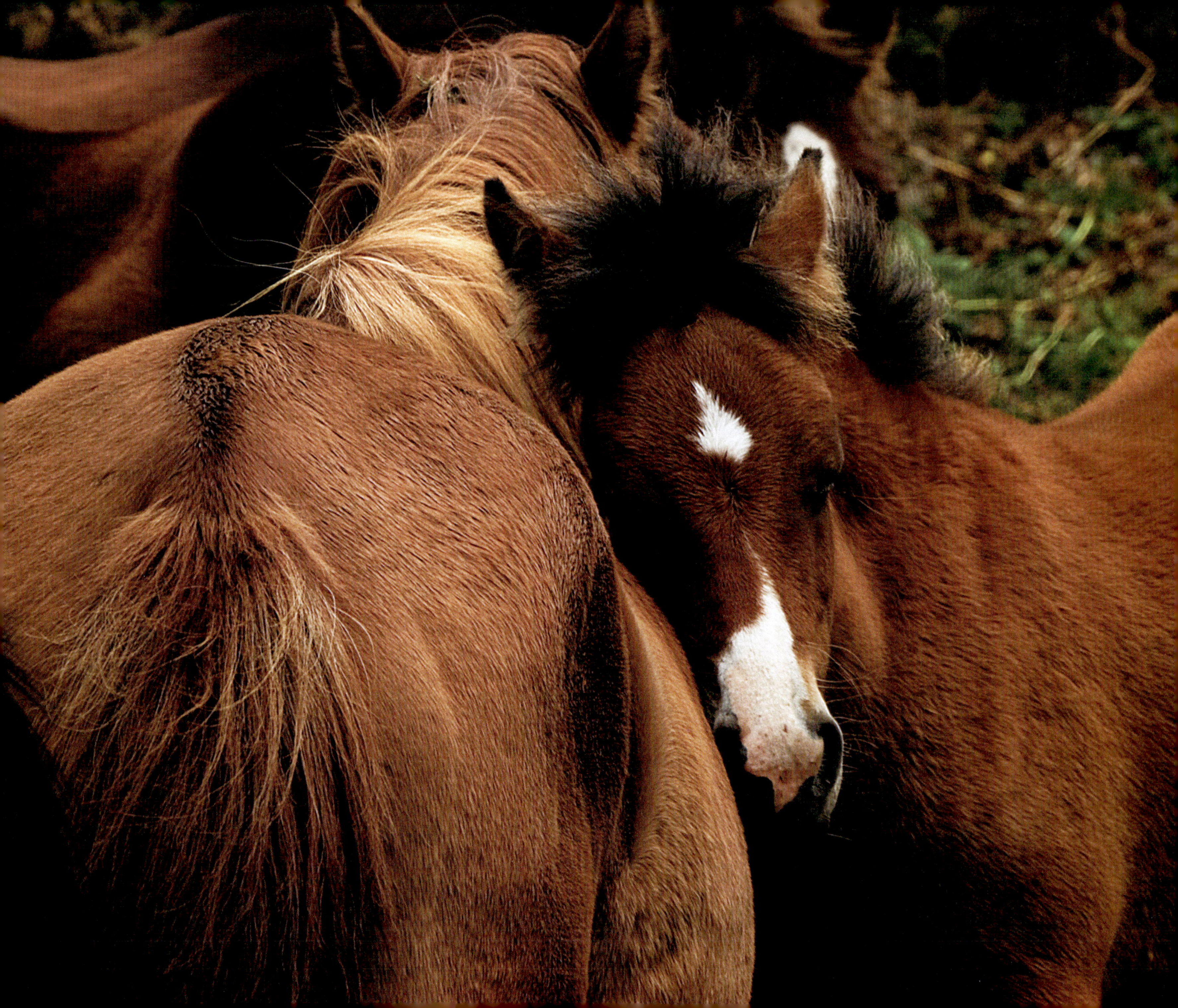

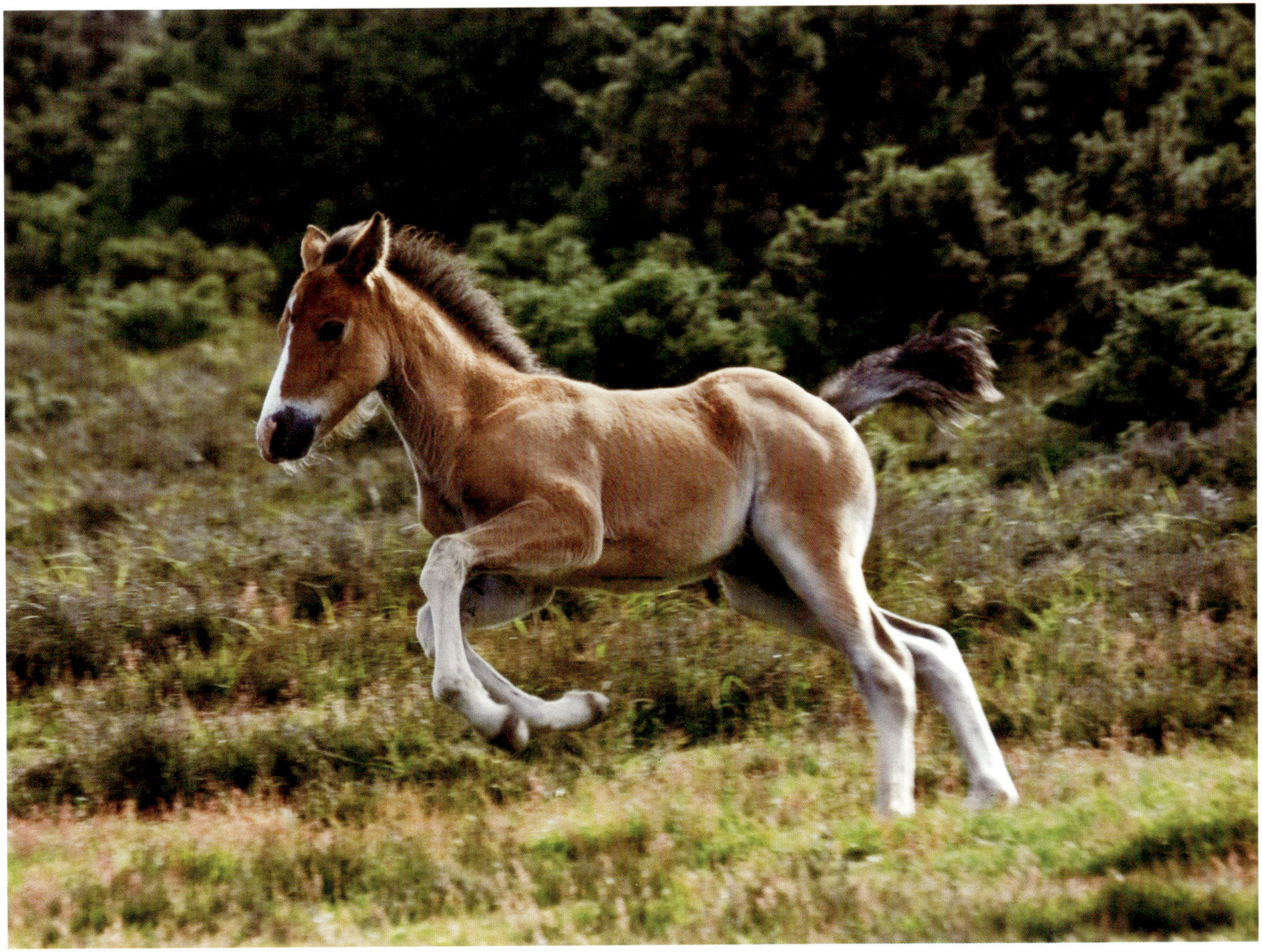

Opposite Mare and foal relaxing after the Ashurst drift, 2005.
Above Tilebarn Peter the Prince on Setley, 2008.

Forest Roads

The stock has right of way out on the open Forest. When an animal chooses to cross a road, it still has right of way and it is the drivers' responsibility to respect the animals.

Sadly, most weeks there are animal fatalities on Forest roads. Those that survive being hit by a car, often have to be destroyed by the Agister and the owner informed. This is a very difficult part of the Agister's job. There are many Hit and Run drivers, causing some animals a painful and lingering death. Surprisingly the largest percentage of accidents involve local drivers who should know better. There is a 40mph maximum speed limit in the Forest but, regrettably not all drivers respect it. Indeed they should drive at 10mph or less when there are animals on the road or verges.

In the summer of 1903 the first pony was killed by a hit and run driver—a colt belonging to Mr. Young of the Green Dragon at Brook. Accurate records were not always kept in the early days, but upwards of 10,000 commoners' animals have been killed since that first unfortunate pony in 1903, and that figure does not include those injured.

Incredible suffering must have resulted from these early accidents. It is dreadful enough today when the Agister has to destroy an animal, having been quickly called to the scene by mobile phone. In 1903, a notice of death or injury would have to be conveyed through a passer by or telegram. The Agister then had to cycle or ride across the Forest to deal with the situation. In 1926 the RSPCA supplied the Agisters with humane killers, and in 1936 the Commoners Defence Association paid for telephones in the Agisters' homes.

The Verderers always encourage the police to pursue prosecutions where there is clear evidence that the motorist responsible was driving in an inappropriate manner or

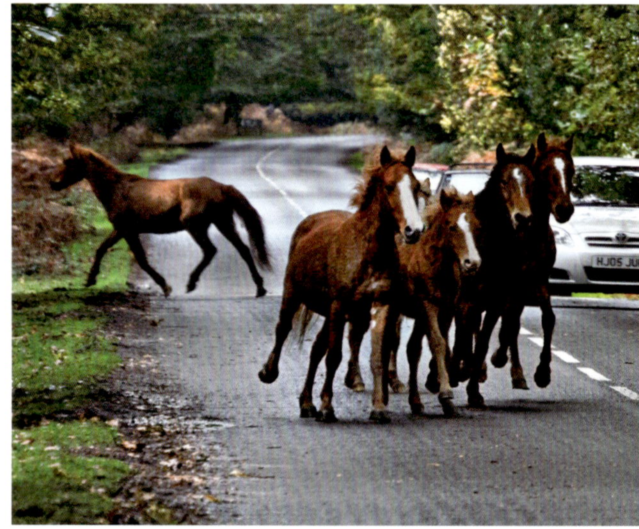

when the driver fails to report the accident to the police. Their Hit and Run Reward Scheme will pay up to £1,000 for information leading to the successful conviction of a driver who fails to report an accident with a Forest animal.

Motorists are rarely prosecuted for injuring or killing an animal unless they fail to report the accident, or there is evidence that their driving fell below an acceptable standard. Hit and Run accidents are taken extremely seriously and drivers who are subsequently identified, will be prosecuted.

All Forest organisations and residents would echo the words of the New Forest Trust: "Enjoy the beauty of our Forest. Please drive safely within the speed limit and respect the animals and countryside code. Be tolerant of our animals and allow them to continue their work as 'architects of the forest', which they have done for the past thousand years".

Above Ponies on the road at Ladycross, 2008.
Opposite A curious Tilebarn Mary Magdalene approaches a car, unaware of the dangers of traffic, 2005.

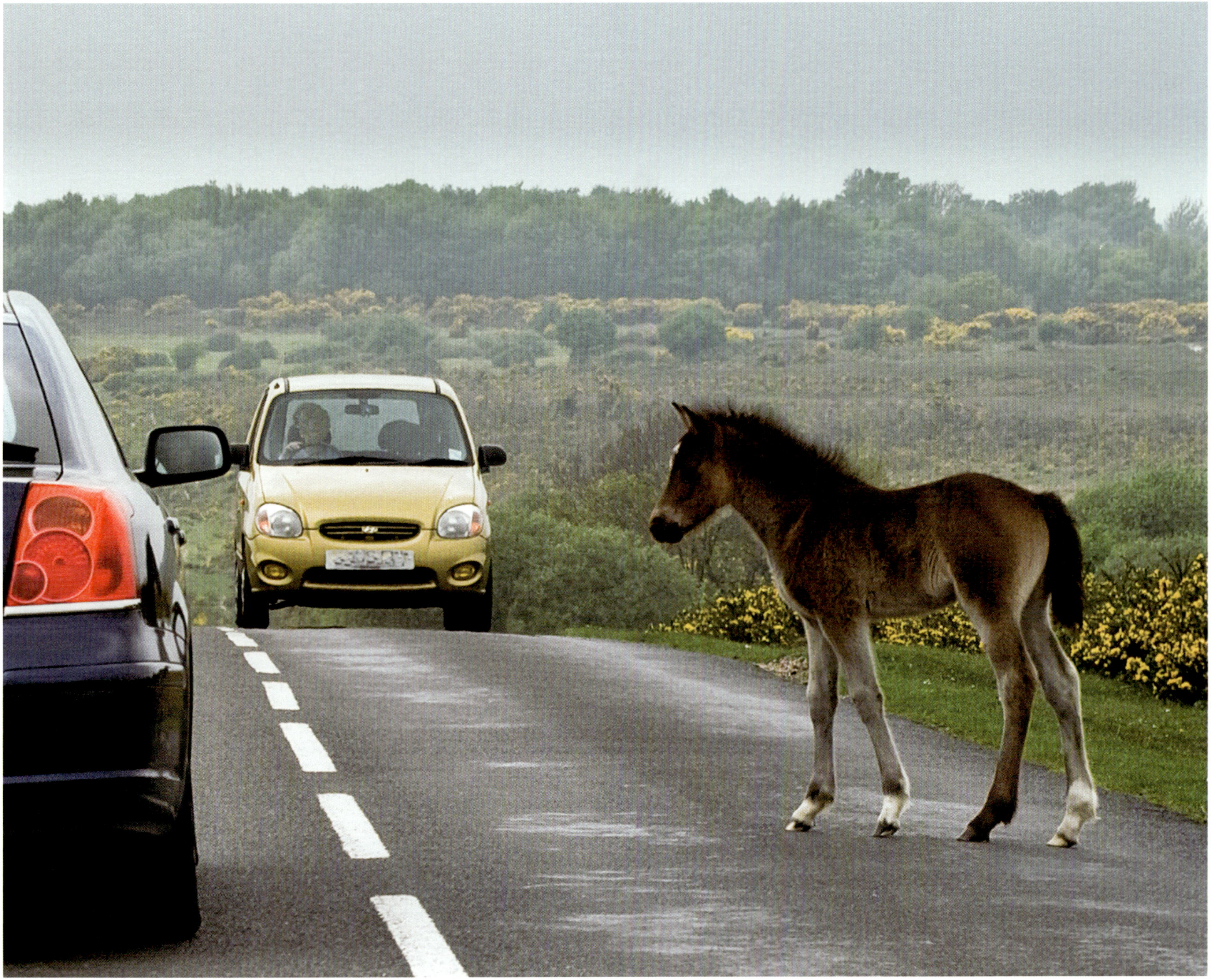

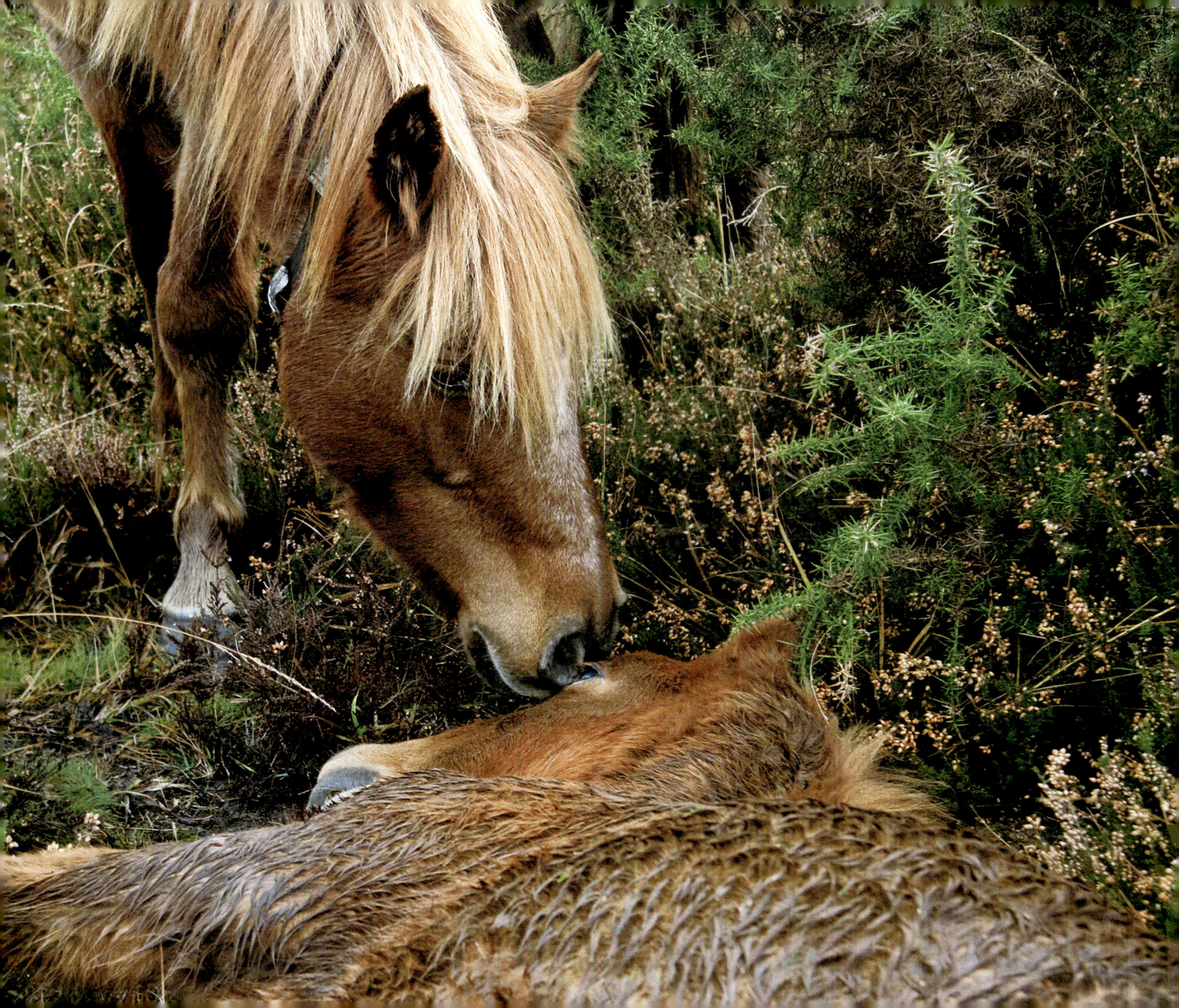

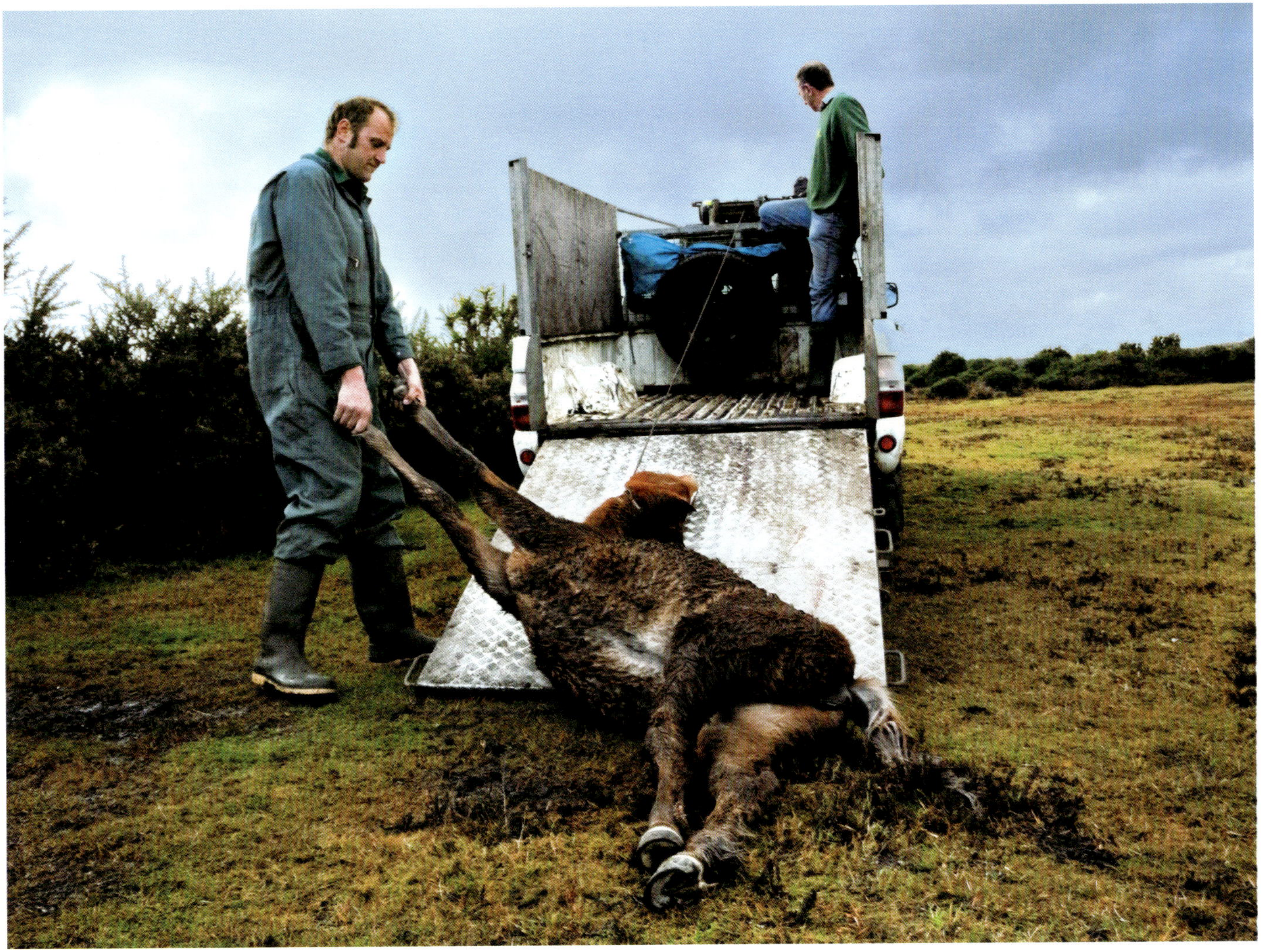

Opposite Lucky Lane Kathleen sniffed her dead foal Bunty and screamed. Bunty's leg was badly broken by a careless driver in broad daylight when she crossed the road to feed from her mother. Agister Robert Maton had to humanely destroy her, 2008.
Above Robert Maton helps Paul Woodhouse from New Forest Hounds' Kennels load Bunty onto his vehicle whilst her mother Kathleen watches, 2008.

New Forest Hounds

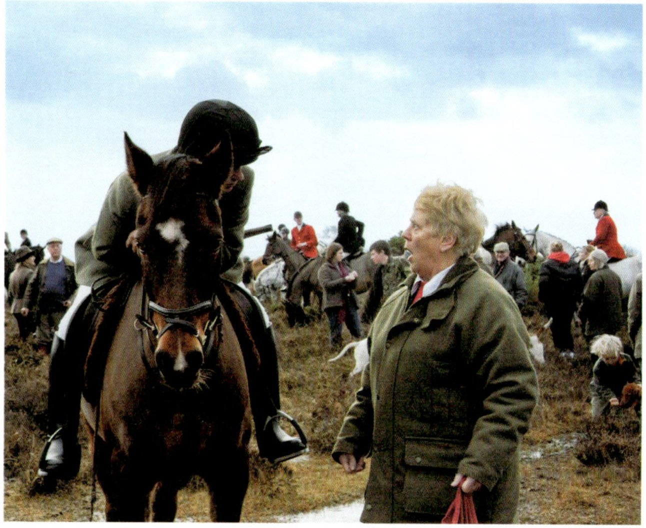

The greatest cause of death for Forest animals is careless drivers. The Kennels of the New Forest Hounds collect commoners' dead animals and dispose of them by feeding the majority of the carcasses to the hounds. Commoning cannot survive without this vital service. The Kennels pick up approximately 95% of all fallen stock on the Forest, which is a unique and environmentally friendly service. It uses living organisms (hounds) to remove biological waste (fallen stock) which if left would be dangerous to humans and the environment due to pathogens. Anything that by law cannot be fed to the hounds is incinerated.

Above New Forest Hounds at Rowbarrow, lead by huntsman Mike Woodhouse. Most of the field are commoners including Bob Garrett The Whip. The trail layer (on foot) Will Day hacks with the hounds to the next location where a new trail will be laid, 2008.
Opposite The New Forest Hounds meet is always very social, 2009.
Following left Commoner Mark Francis trail hunting with the NF Hounds, 2009.
Following right Details of drift preparations.

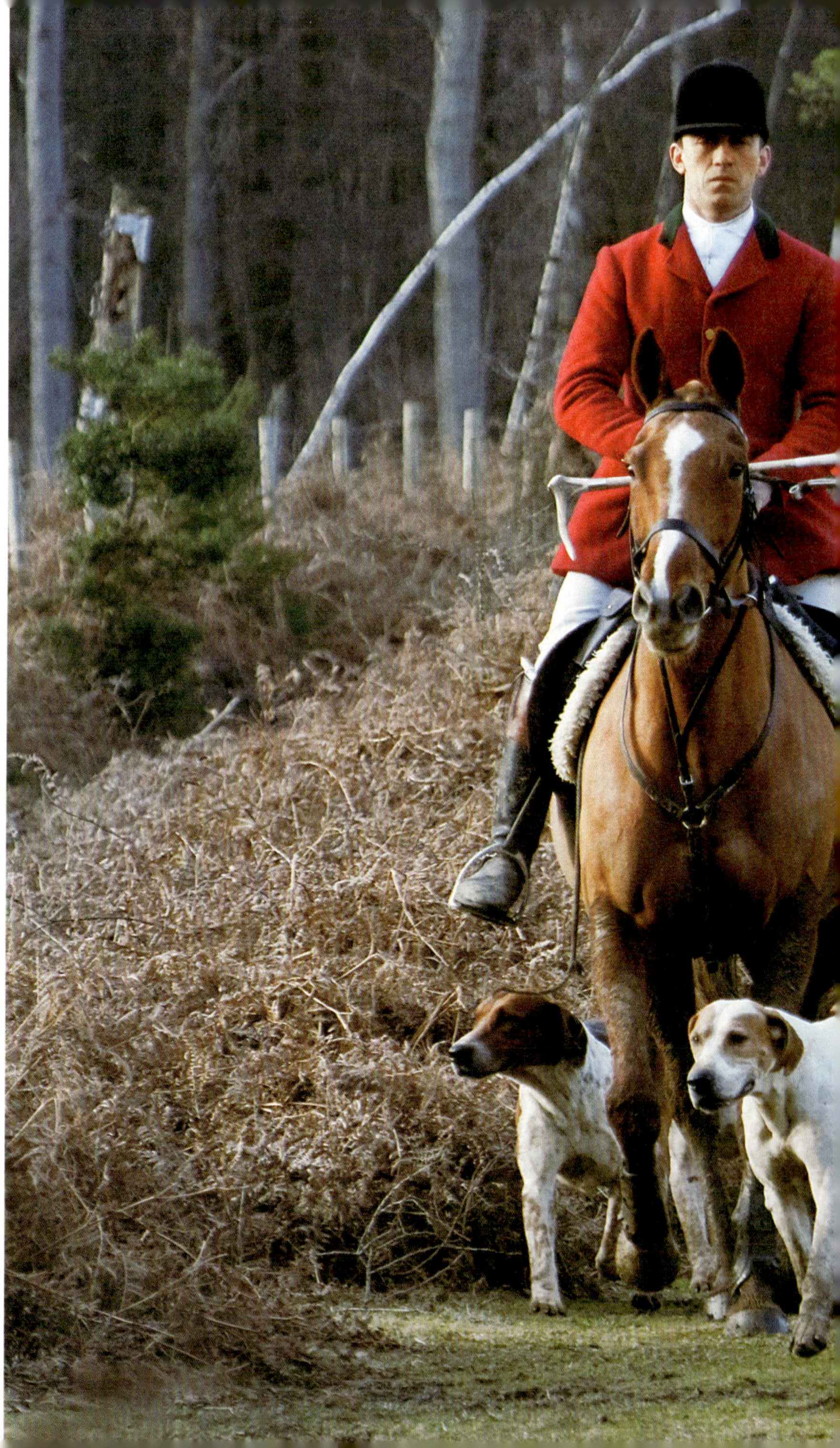

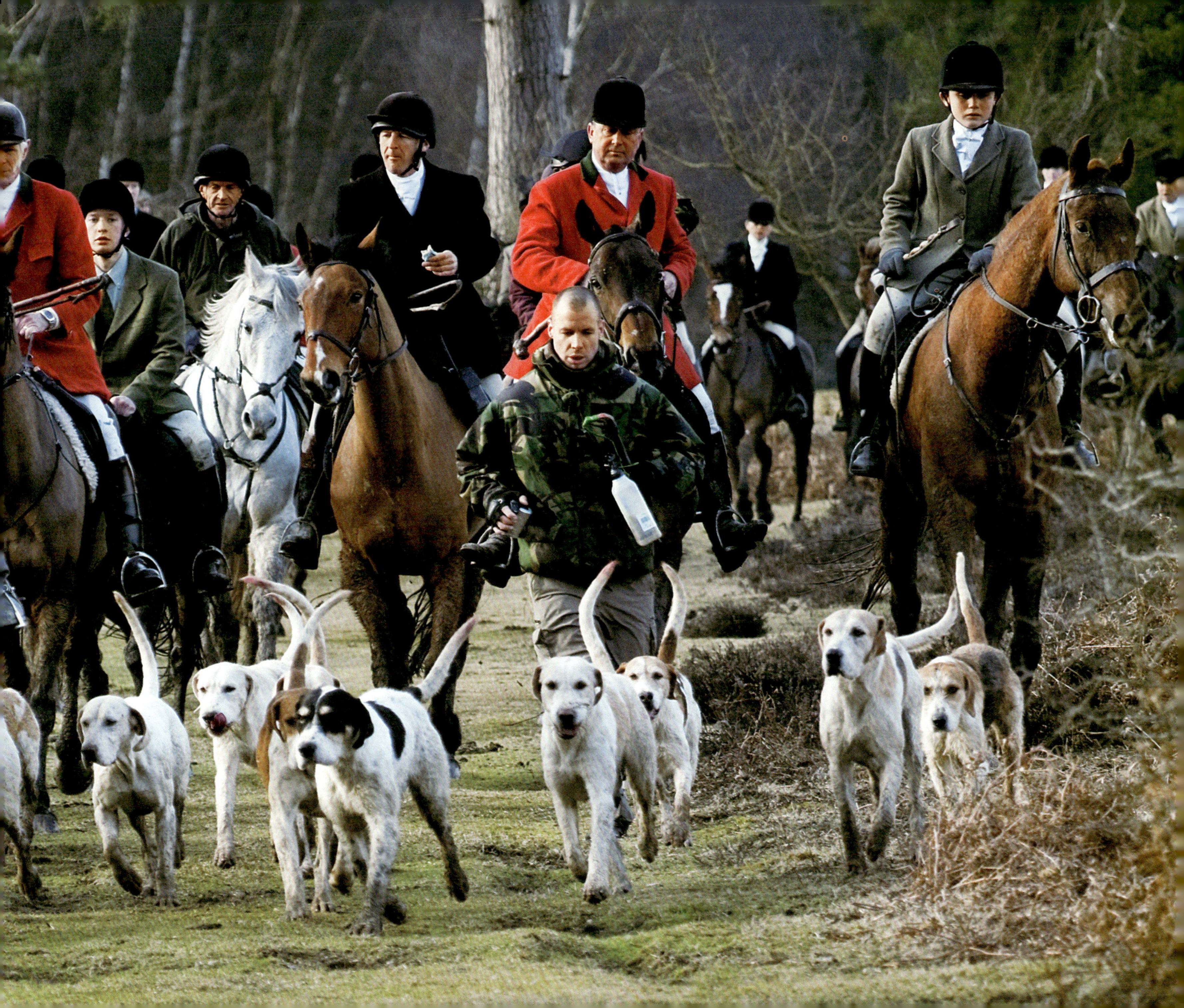

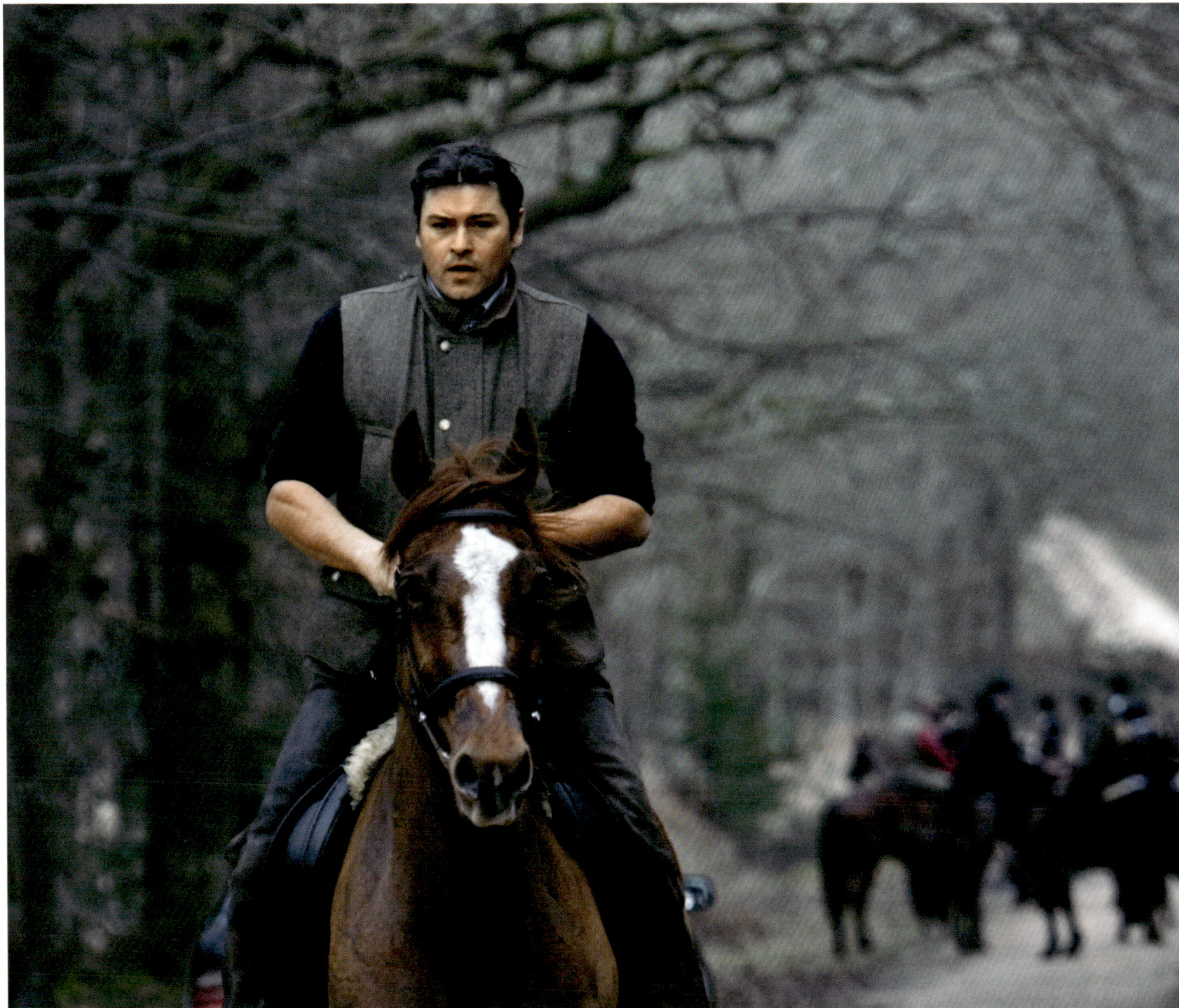

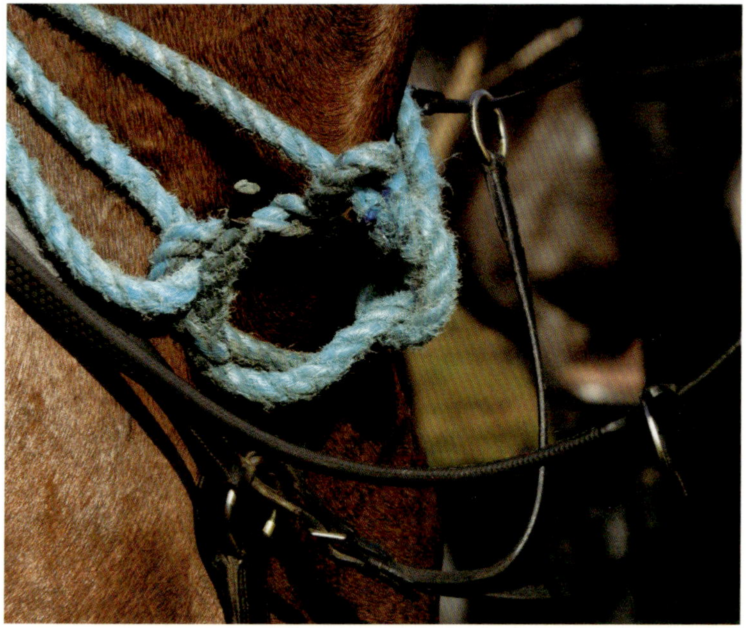
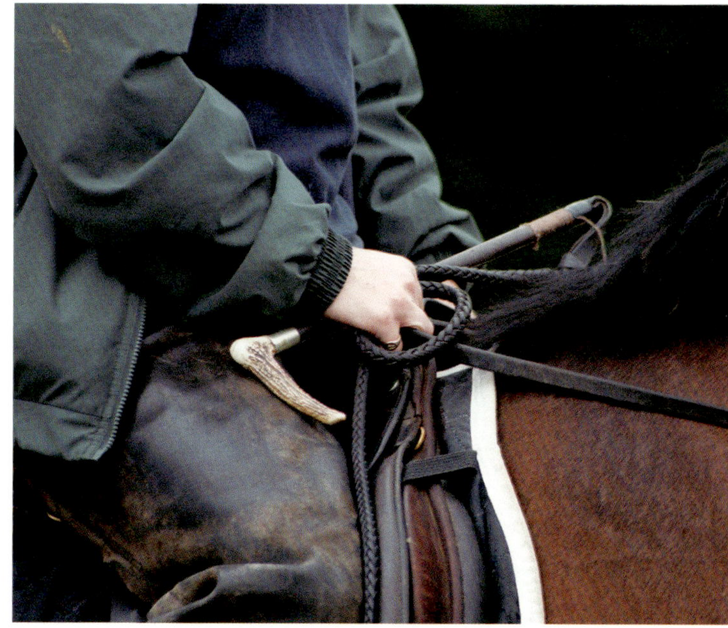
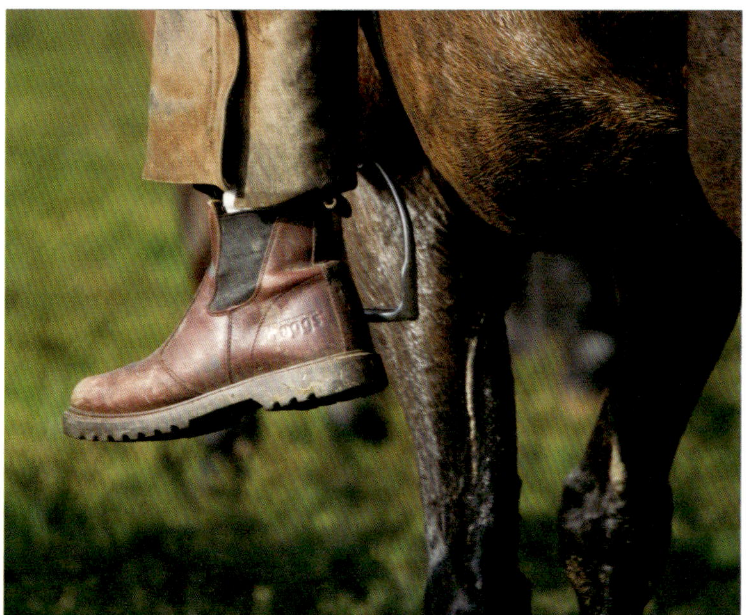
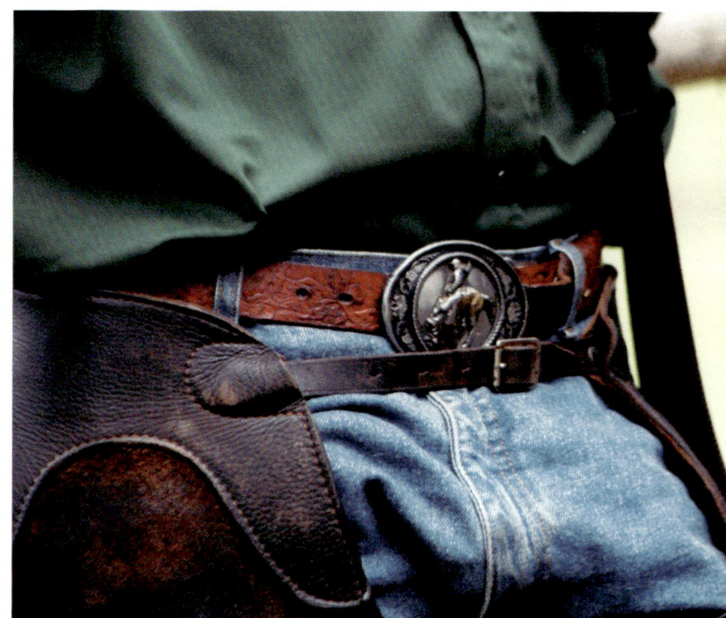

Pony Drifts

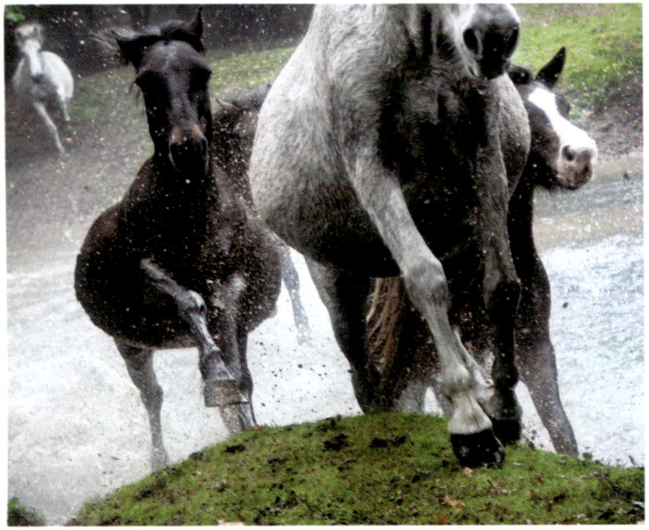

New Forest ponies run wild on the Forest but they are all owned by commoners. Once a year it is essential that all the stock is rounded up for health checks, for marking and to wean the foals that have been born on the Forest. This is the time when surplus stock is removed from the Forest and taken to the sales. The round-ups, organised by the Agisters, are called pony drifts. There are usually about 40 drifts during late summer and early autumn.

For each drift, the Agister formulates a plan with his commoners, deciding from which direction to approach the ponies. The riders distribute themselves accordingly and the walkers (commoners on foot) are positioned in likely escape routes. The riders must have an intimate knowledge of the Forest as the drifts move at great speed and taking a wrong turning or having to negotiate a bog during a drift could destroy a day's work. The expertise of the riders and

Above Ponies coming through the water at New Park, 2008.
Opposite Colin Moore expertly bringing in a mare and foal at Ipley, 2005.

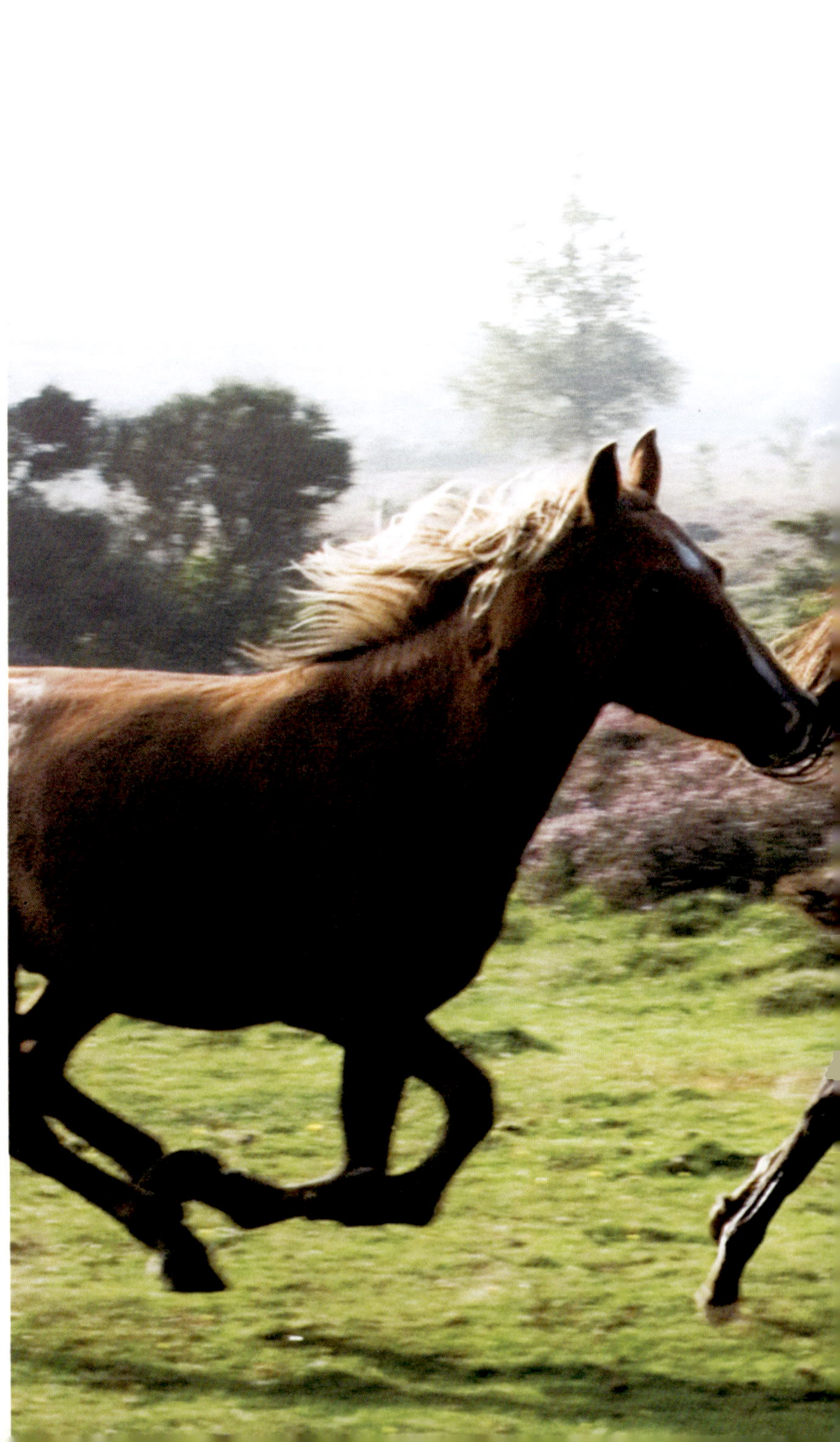

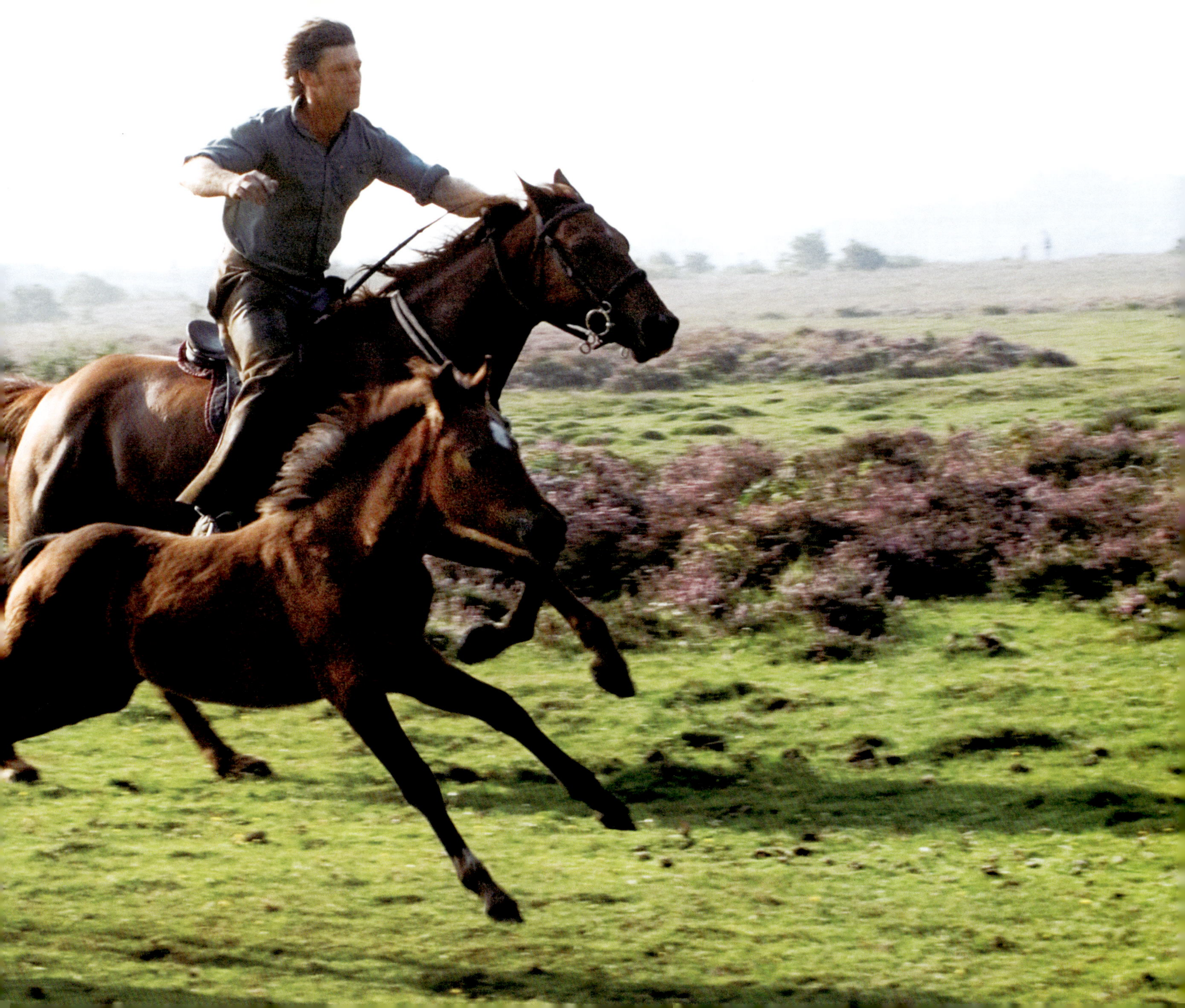

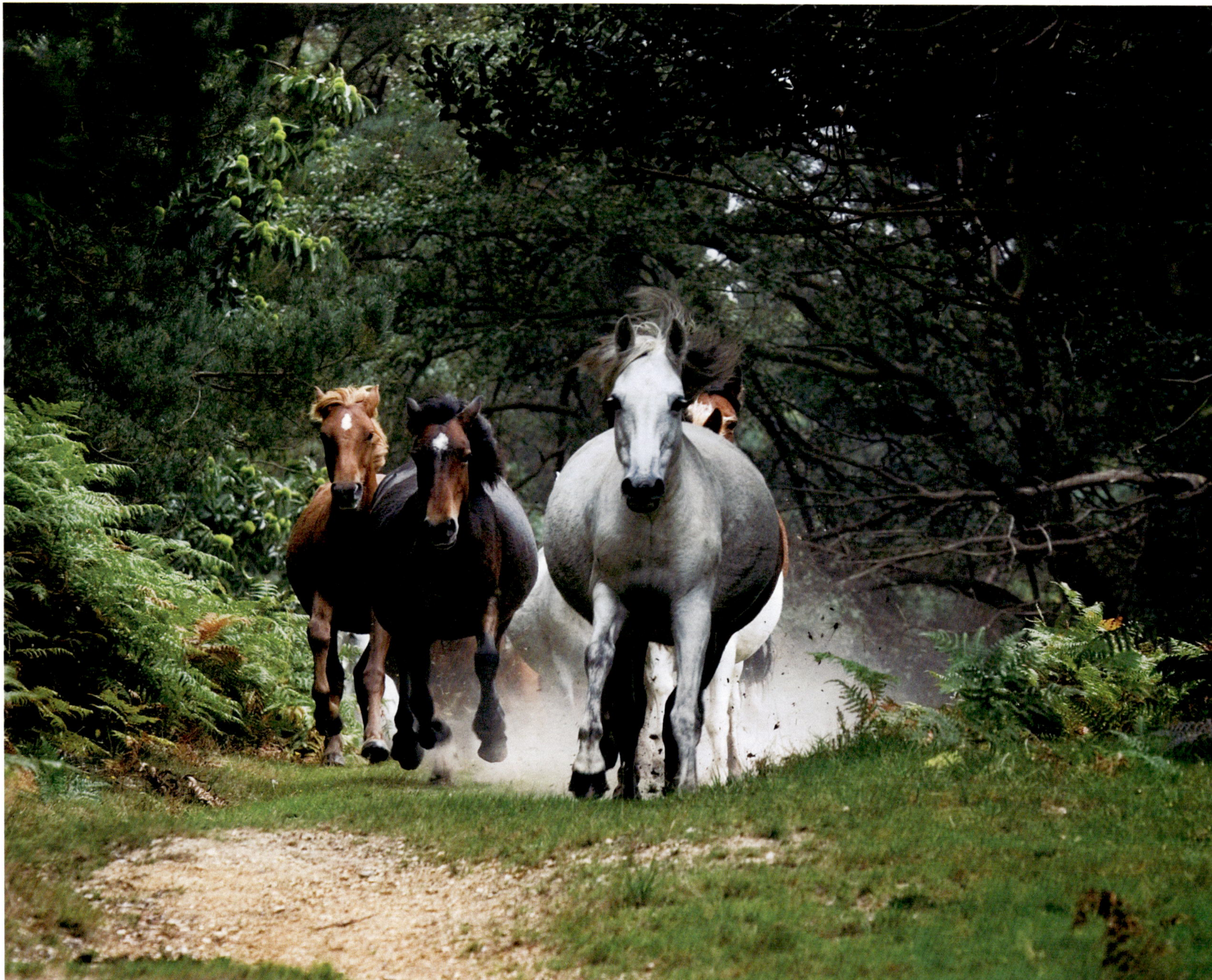

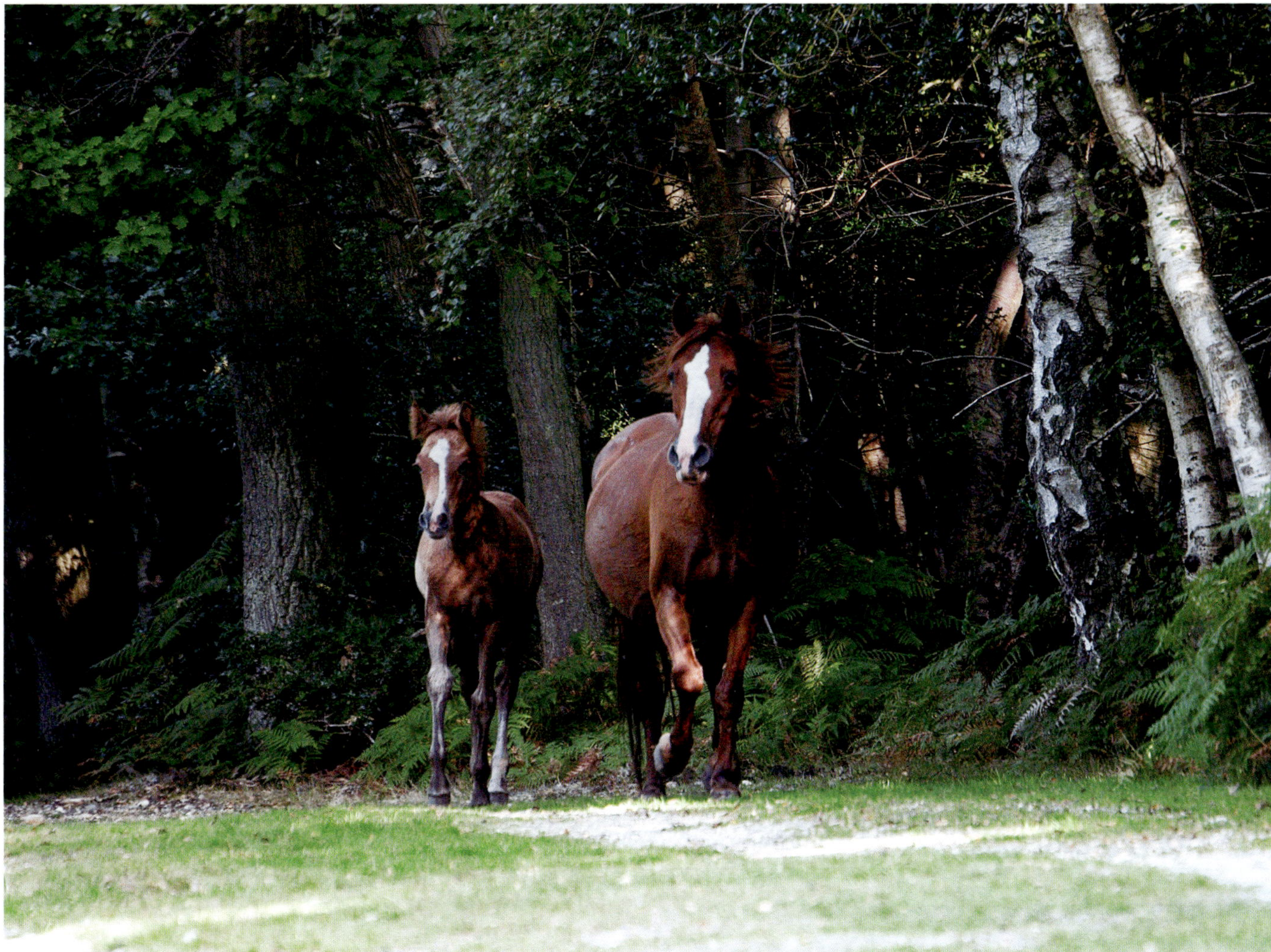

Opposite Ponies coming down the driftway at Broomy, 2005.
Above Mare and foal coming down the driftway at Hilltop, 2005.

the agility of their horses justly commands great respect.

The drift is a magnificent sight with up to a hundred ponies at a time moving across the Forest at full gallop. The pace at which the ponies are driven is breath-taking and the ride can be hazardous even though the riders are as skilled in the saddle as any cowboy.

New Forest ponies move at great speed and have extraordinary stamina. They can go like the wind. At the start of the drift, some will take off at a fast gallop and can cover a couple of miles before giving in and being guided into the pound. Others will slow down after half a mile or so and allow themselves to be gently trotted in.

The wild ponies have the advantage over the riders. They can cross a bog at great speed, but the pursuing pony with a rider on board may find it impassable or the pony—and rider—can end up in the bog.

New Forest ponies are sure-footed riding ponies. They know exactly what they are doing and can turn very quickly. If a commoner is mounted on one when drifting, he or she can 'go out the side door' very easily if they don't hang on tight.

Only bone-fide practising commoners are allowed to ride on the drifts. They are working days, and riders who are not experienced in the art of drifting can get in the way, and could lose the Agister's whole day's work. The Verderers and Agisters strongly discourage the public from attending the drifts, which is for their own safety.

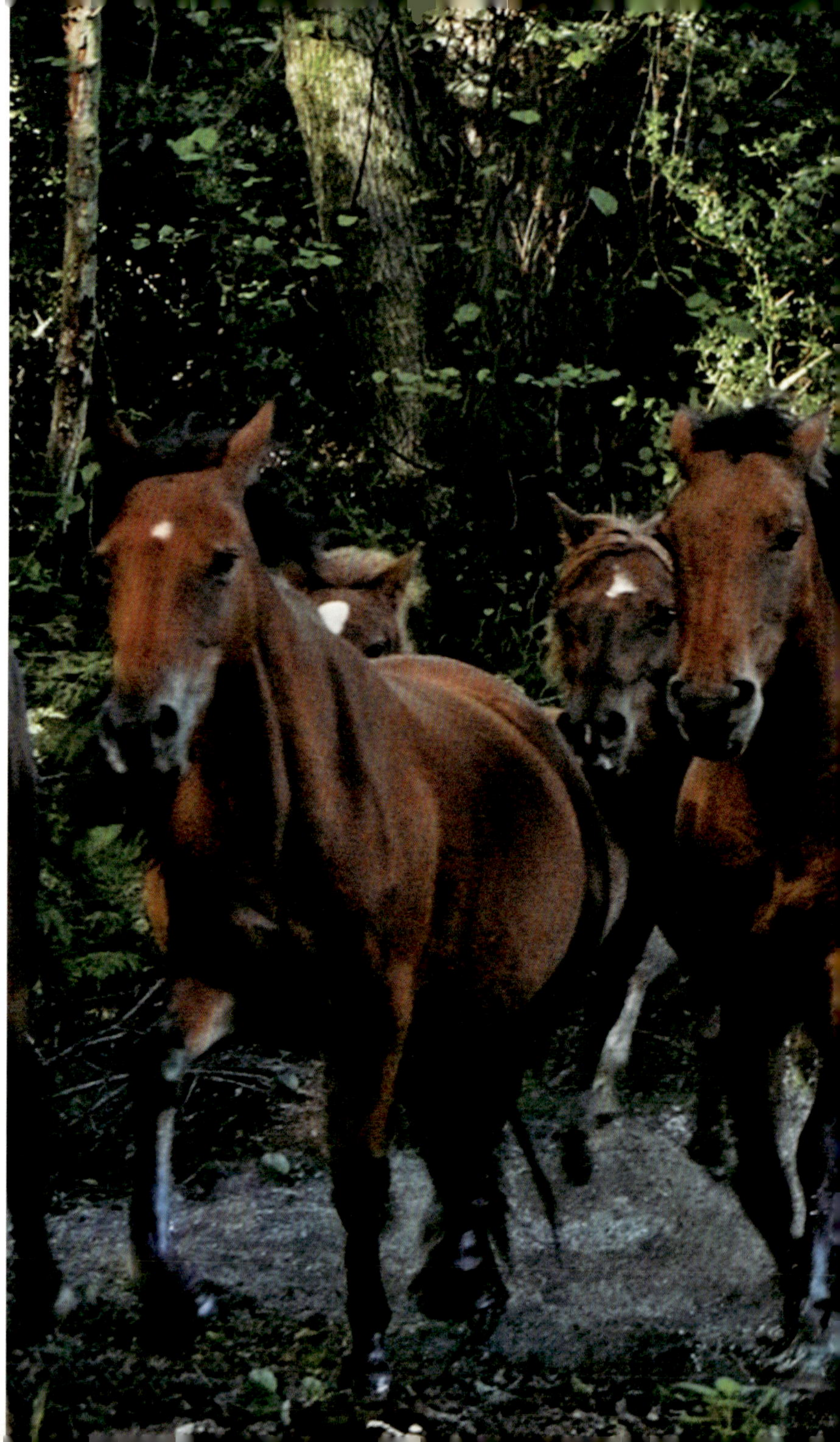

New Forest Ponies coming through the water at Culverley, 2005.

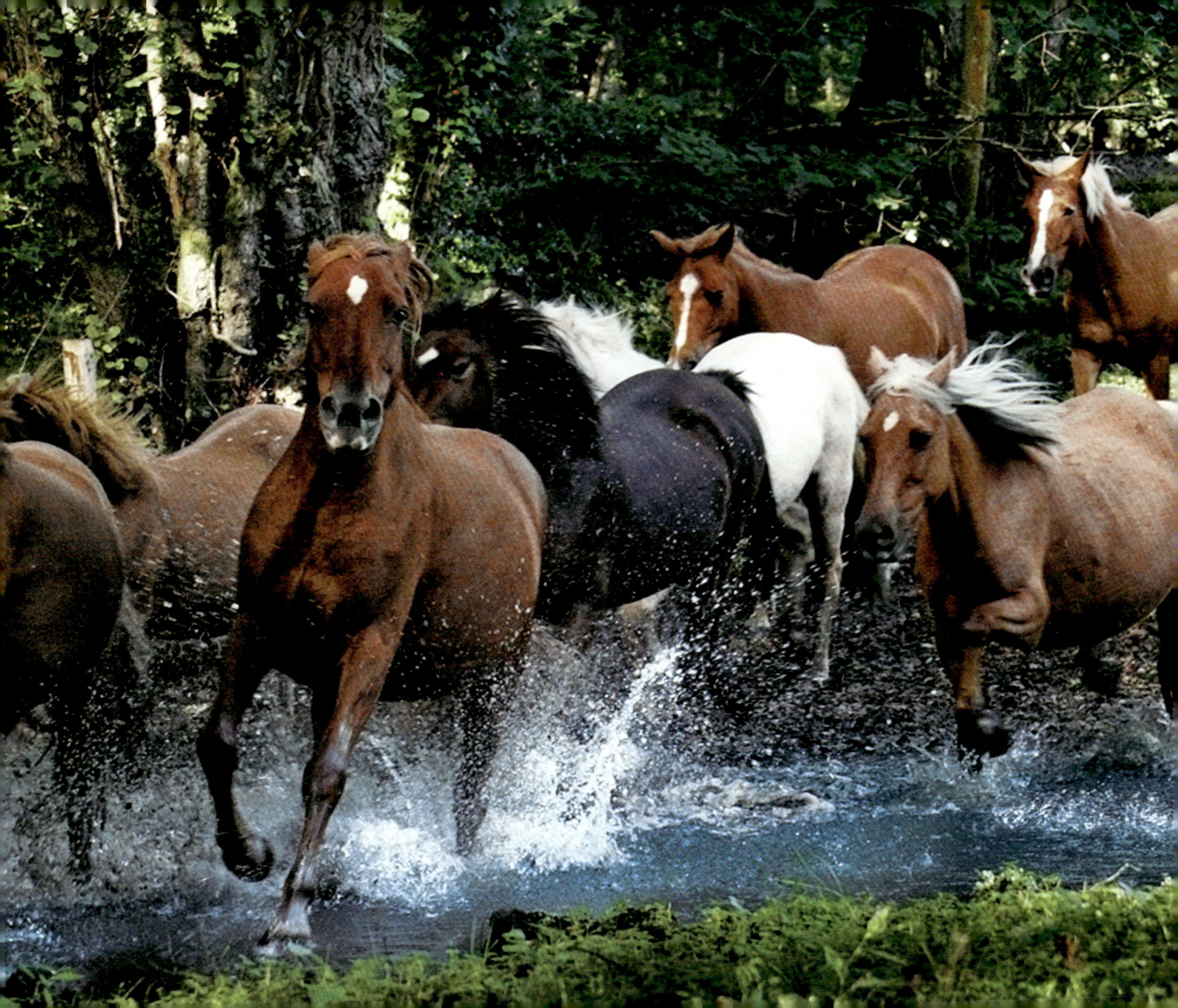

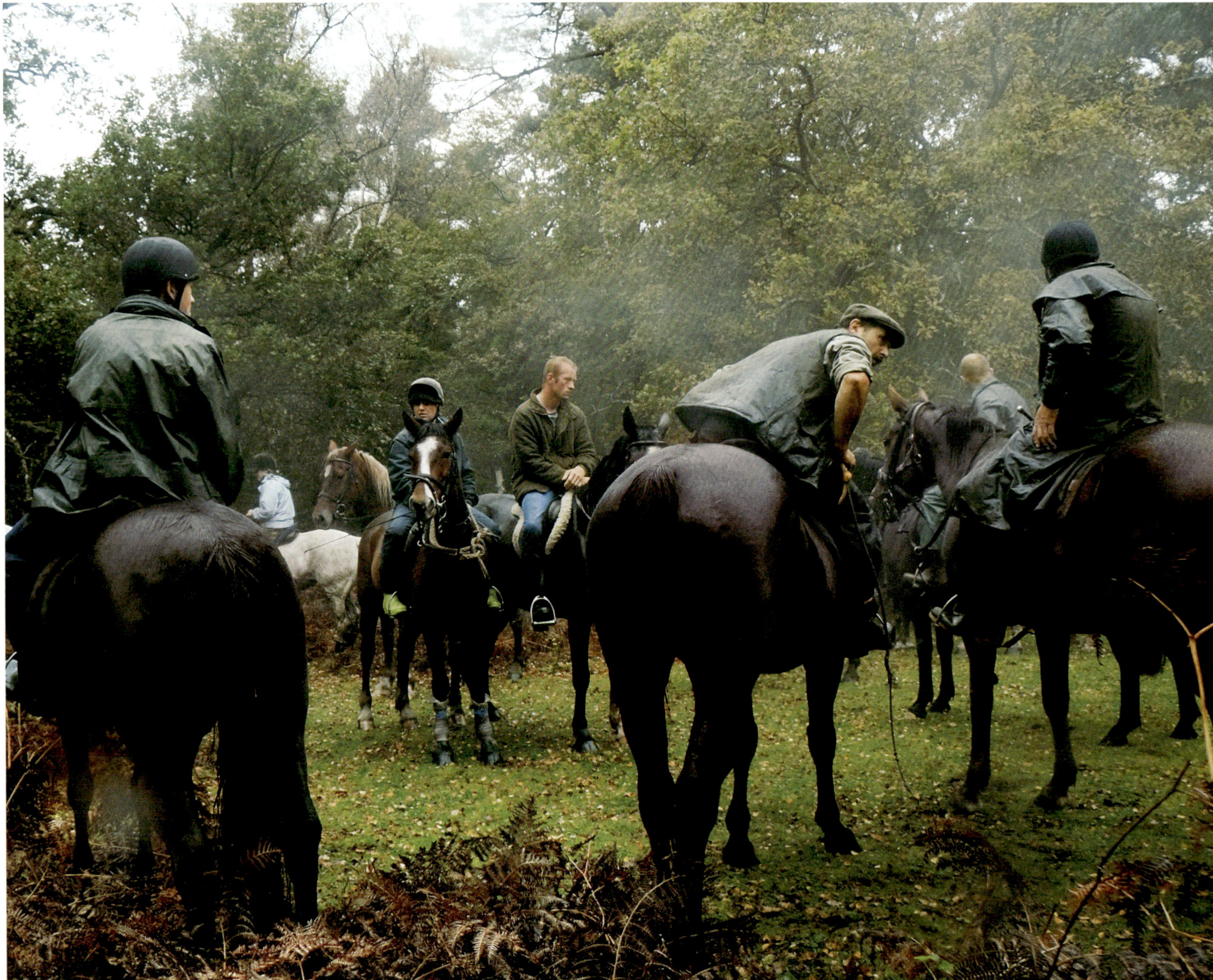

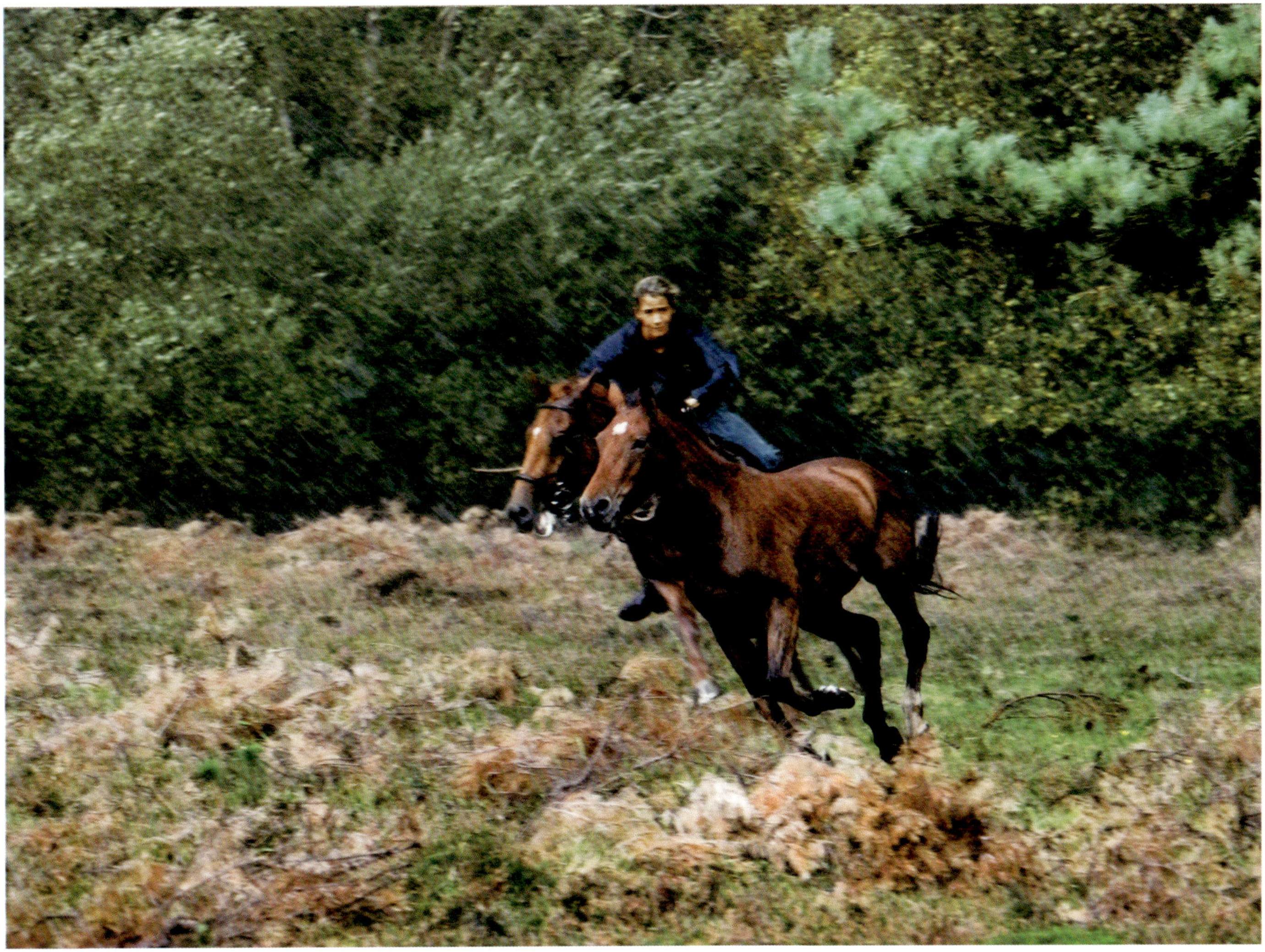

Opposite Drifts happen in all weathers, Commoners pause to discuss their next move in the woods near Furzey Lodge, 2008.
Above Despite driving rain Beth Stride brings in a mare needed by the owner, at Ashurst, 2006.

In the Pound

On a good day, a drift will bring in around 100 ponies. Once the Agister in charge of the drift has brought in all the ponies he can, he informs the mounted commoners and the walkers. They check that everybody who started out with them has returned and if someone is missing, the Agister sends out a search party.

The ponies are firmly secured in the pound. There is much excitement discussing the drama of the morning but there is still work to be done and the fire is prepared immediately for the branding irons.

As soon as they have taken care of the needs of their saddle horses, the commoners move to the pound to look for their ponies. There may be some surprises: a mare that hasn't been seen for several years may suddenly show up with a beautiful filly foal on her; a favourite mare may be lost and another may come in lame or injured. The ponies are wild and the public are warned to stand clear. The commoners know what they are doing and move expertly between the animals to avoid flying hooves. In order to examine all the stock, they isolate a small number of ponies at a time and drive them into a smaller pound called a crush. The aim is to keep the mares with their foals, but inevitably some get separated and there is often agitated calling from one to the other.

Once in the crush, the Agister moves deftly and quickly amongst the ponies, skillfully cutting or 'marking' their tails, stuffing the hair in his back pocket as he goes. Every pony that comes in on the drift has its tail cut to indicate that the owners have paid the marking fee. Each Agister has his own version of the tail mark and every commoner living in a particular Agister's area will have that Agister's tail mark put into all his animals.

The ponies are inspected by their owners and, if any are in poor condition, they are loaded onto a trailer to be taken back and cared for on the owner's holding. The ponies the owners want to sell at Beaulieu Road are also loaded up. Those foals staying on the Forest are branded, wormed and sometimes given a fluorescent collar to give the animal some protection against night-time traffic.

All ponies that run on the Forest must bear the owner's registered brand. Hot branding is much the cheapest and most satisfactory way of identifying a pony. The foal is held against the edge of the pound by three or four men while its hair—either around the saddle or the shoulder—is clipped out with special scissors and the branding iron applied by the Agister or an experienced commoner. Despite the smell of burning hide and smoke, the job is done so quickly that the foal doesn't realise what has happened.

Drift days can be long days. Whole families participate and the children run around learning the skills. Children are integrated into the commoning community at an early age and many take part in the drifts as soon as they can ride. Most commoning children start their own herd at a very early age.

Commoners looking for their ponies in the pound after the Ipley drift, 2003.

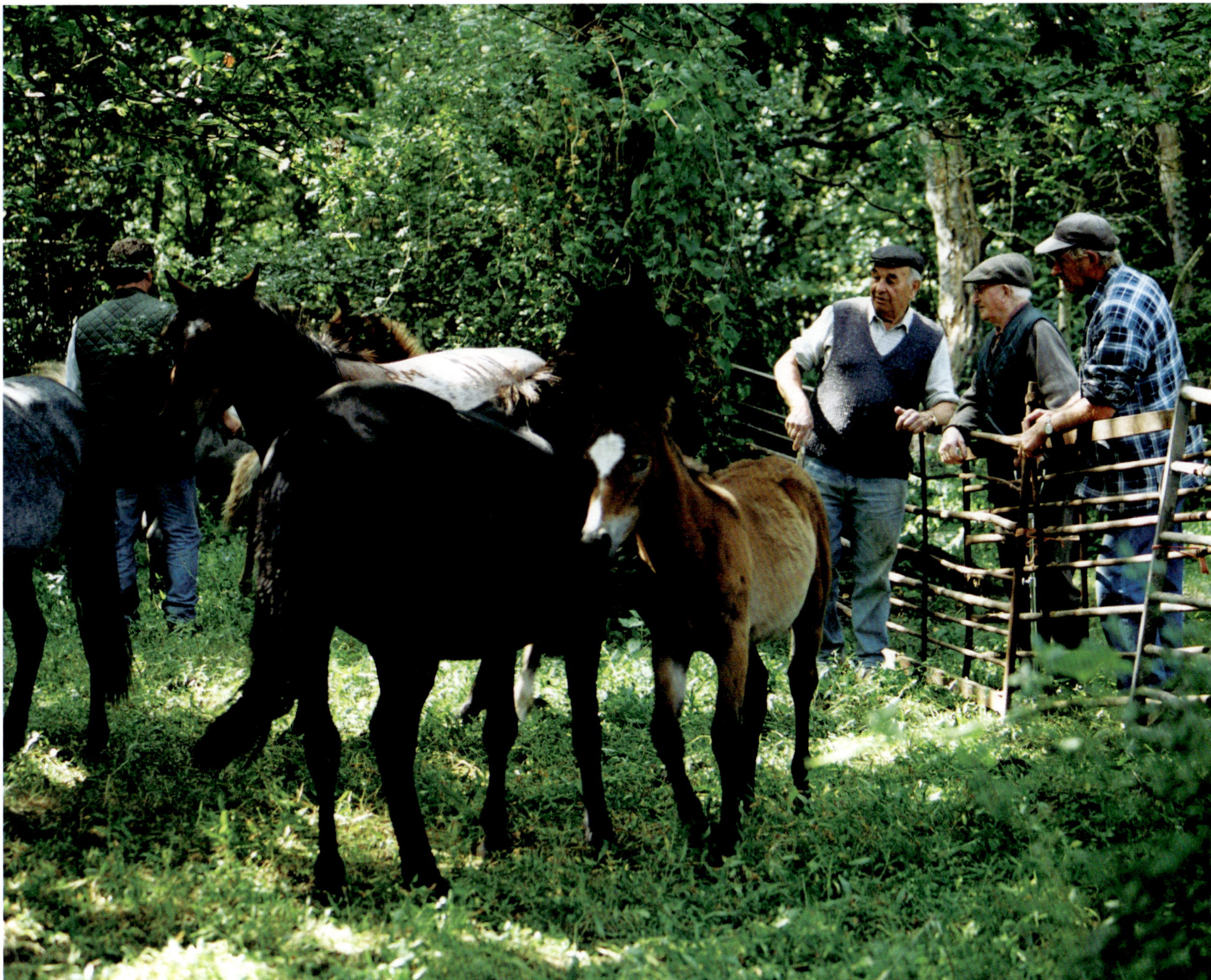

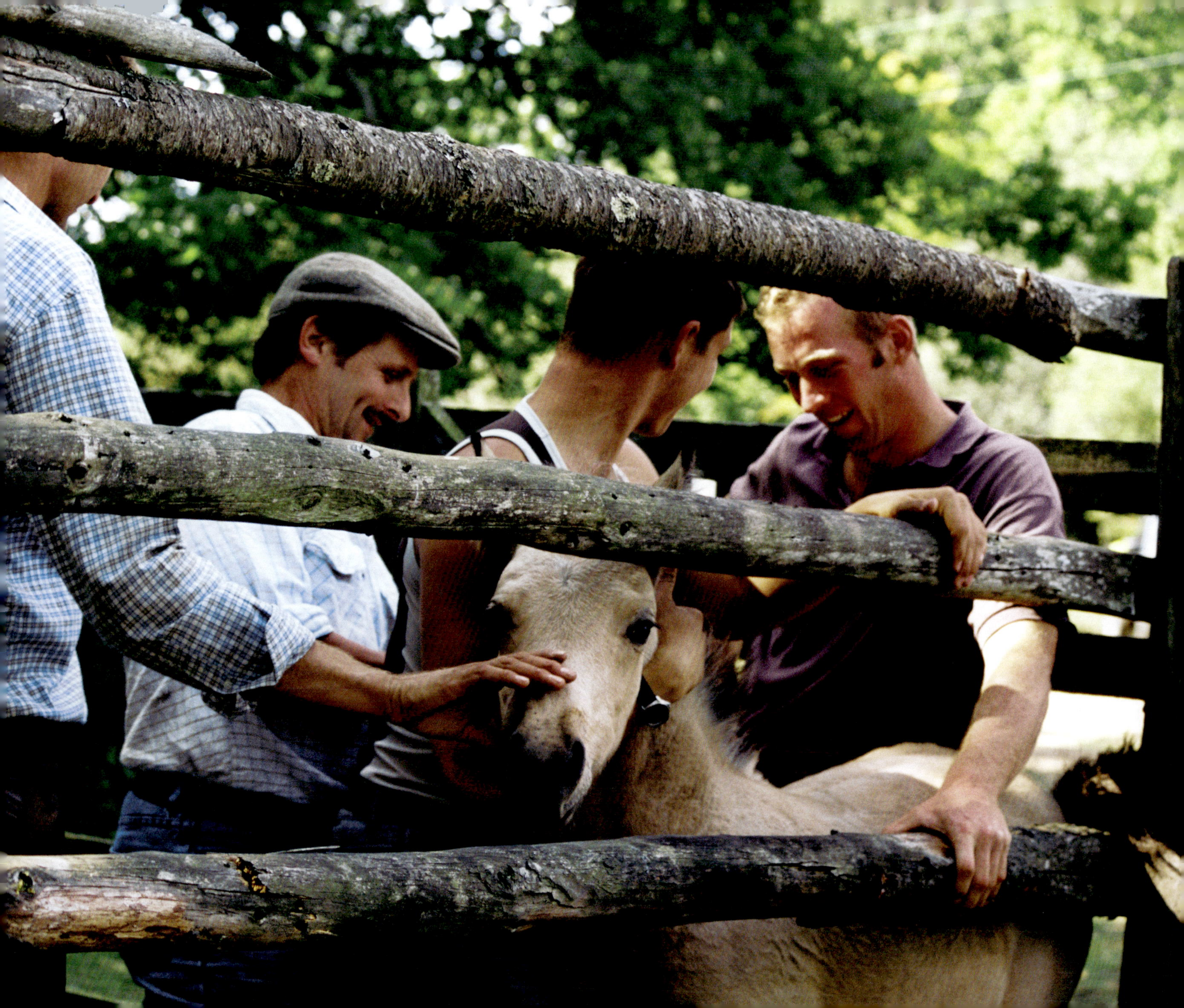

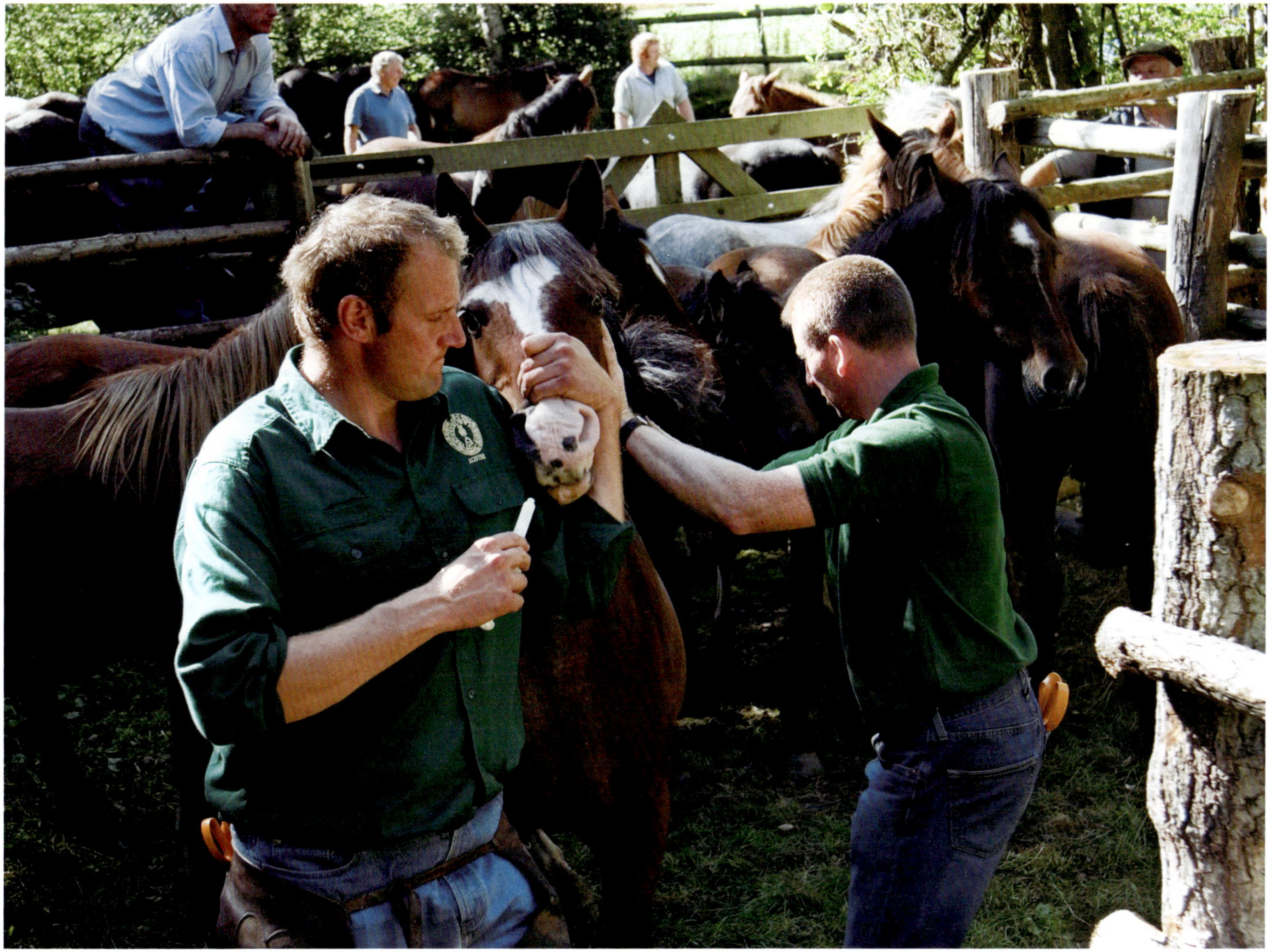

Opposite Michael Maton, Ben Mansbridge and his father Bobby holding a foal in the pound before branding, 2003.
Above Agisters Robert Maton and Mike Lovell worm Pat Dunning's Foxhills Solo in the Weirs pound, 2005.

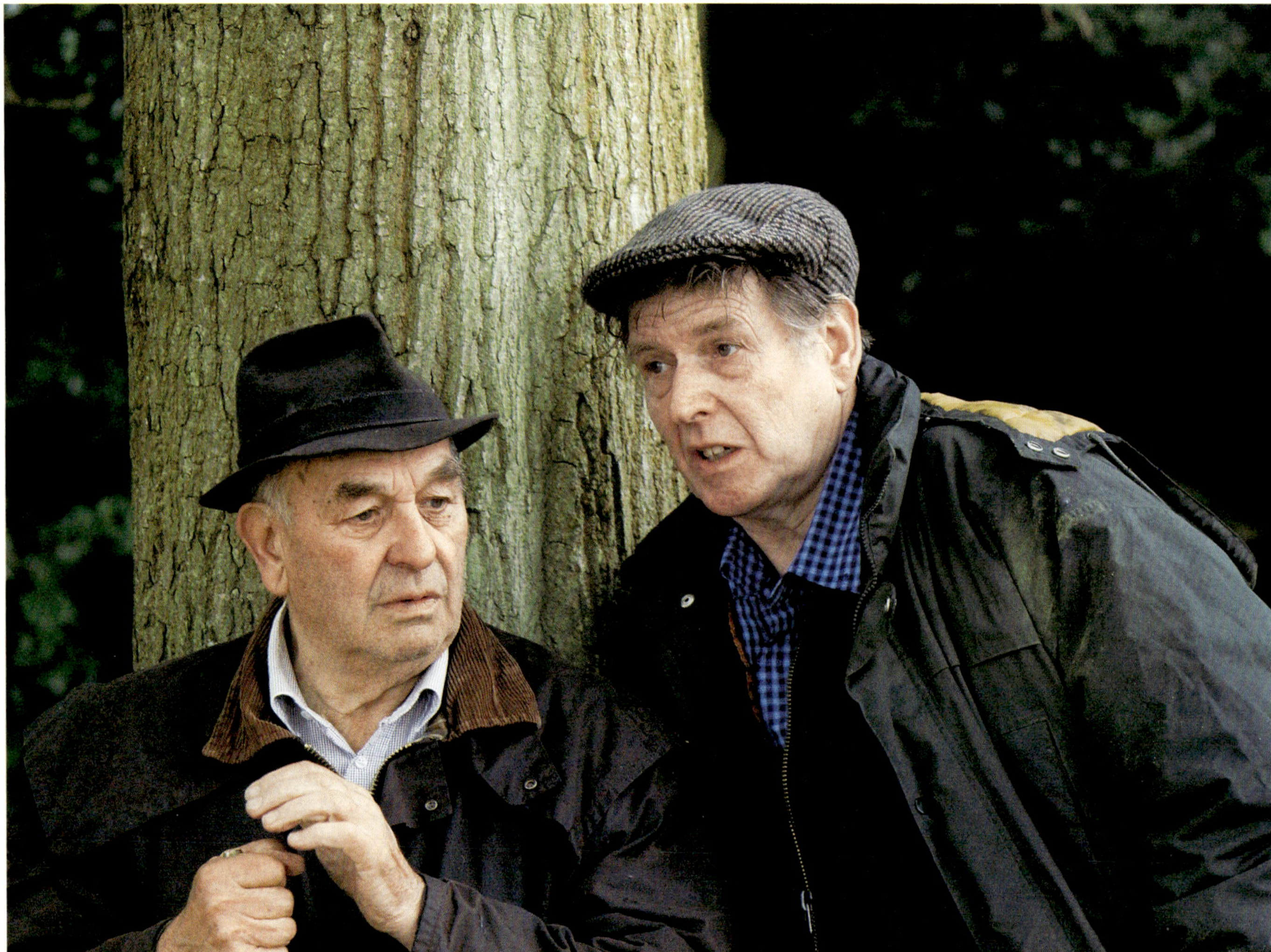

Above Jeff Kitcher (right) tells Ray Readhead an interesting piece of information at Blackfield and Hilltop, 2006.
Opposite Ponies resting after the drift at Blackfield and Hilltop. The fluorescent collar helps to keep them safe on the road at night, 2004.

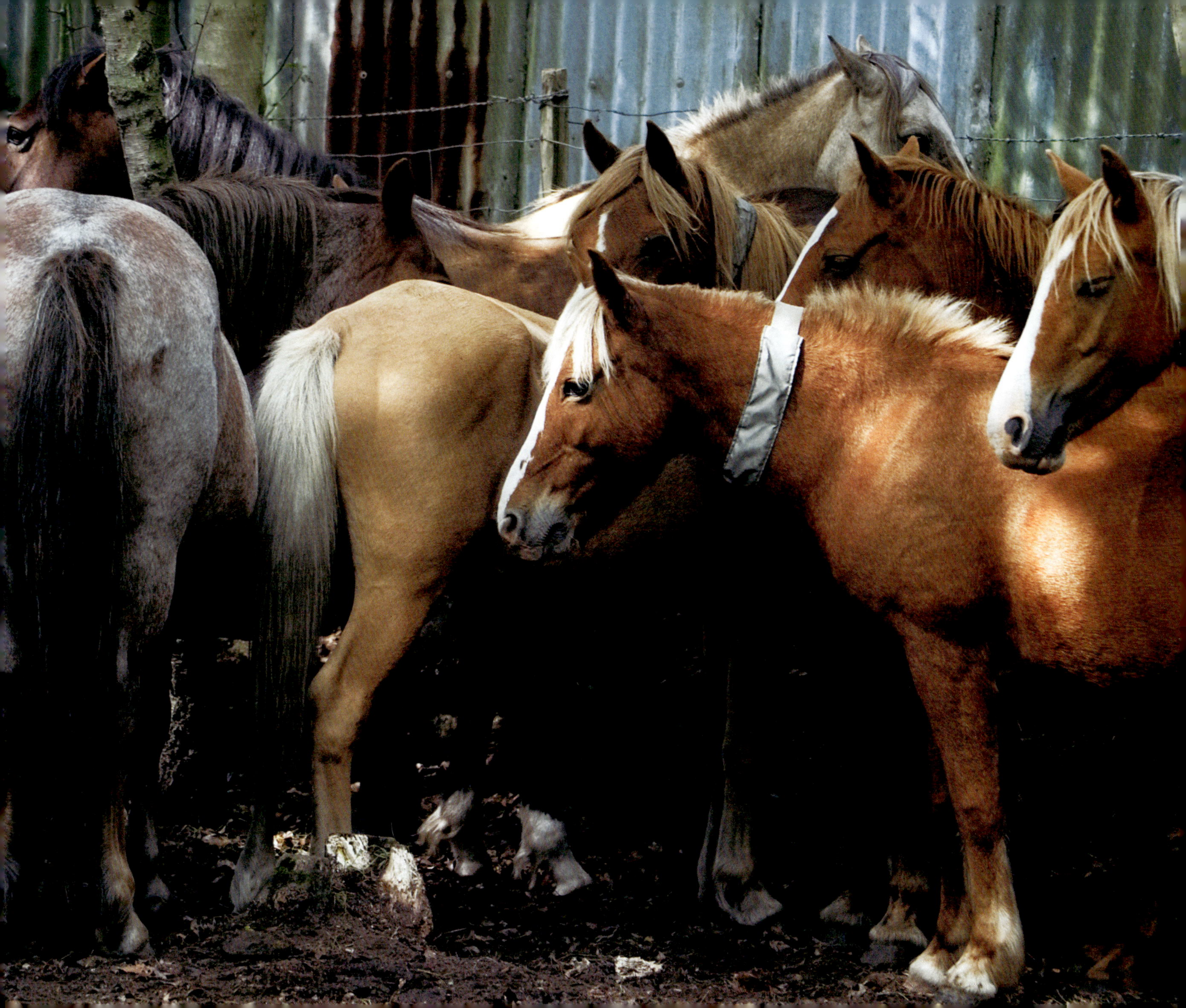

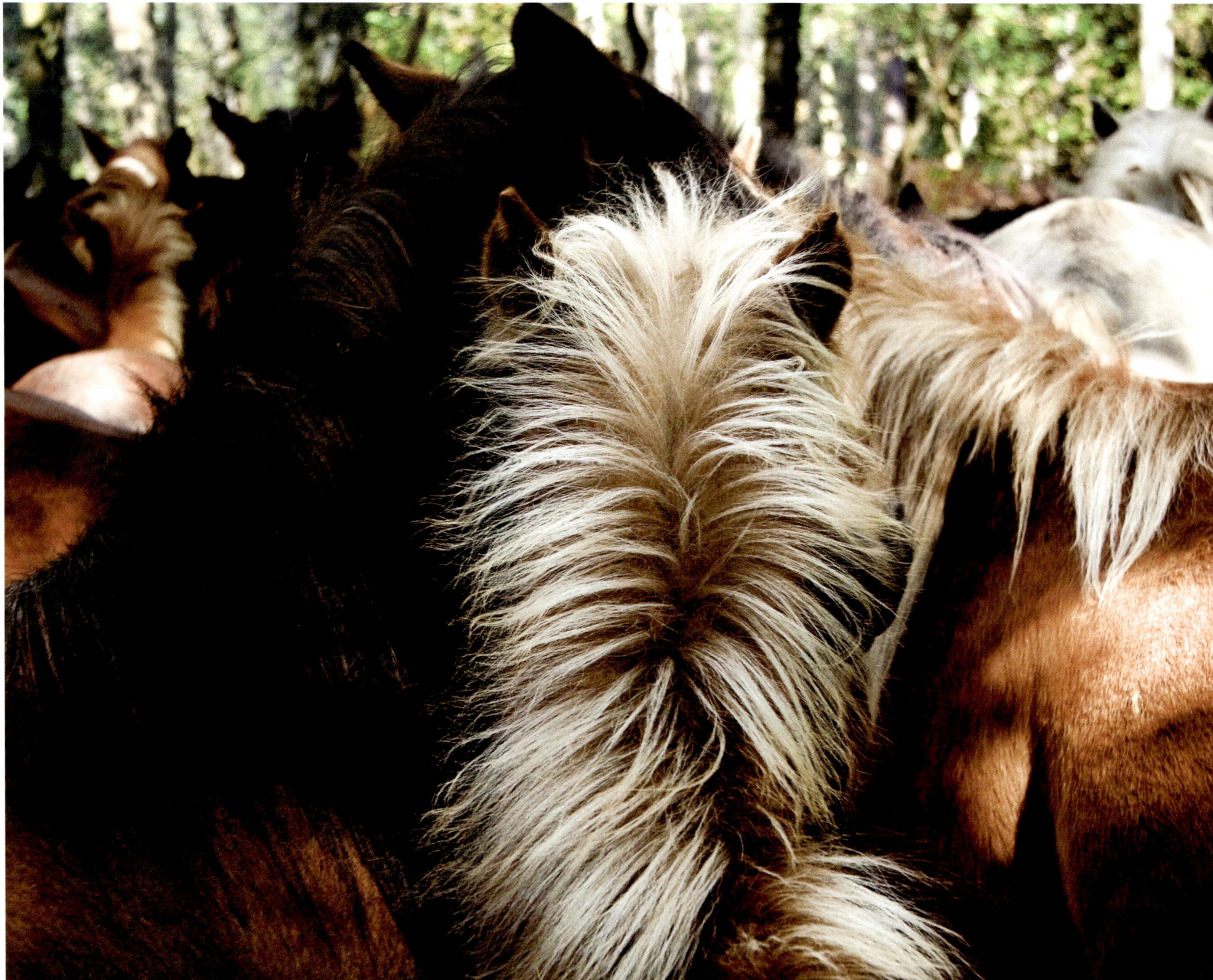

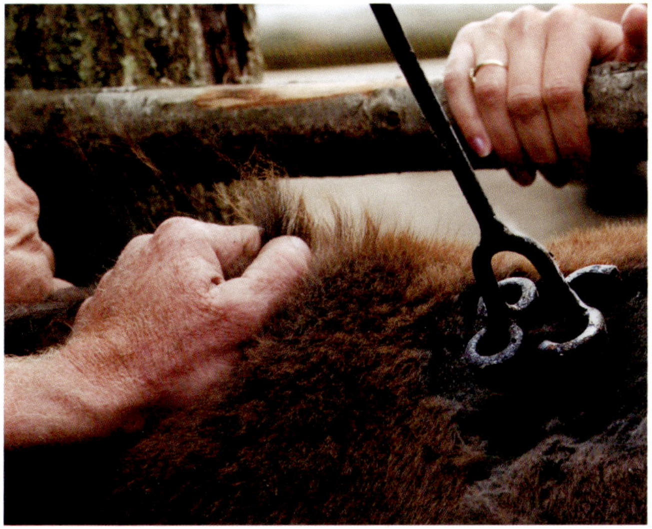

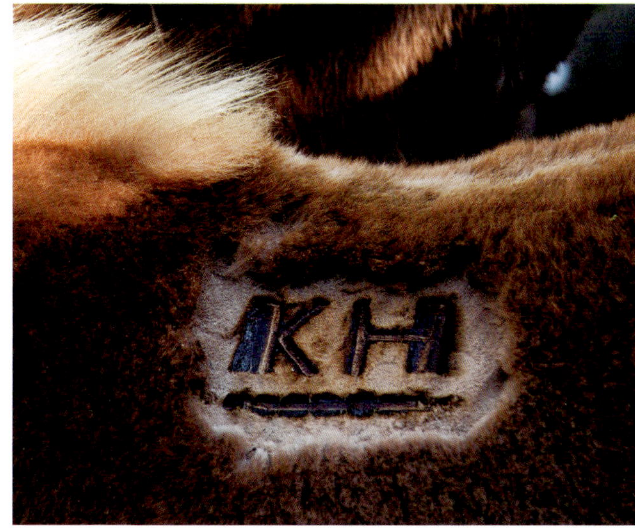

Opposite Ponies in the pounds at Balmer Lawn, 2008.
Above Branding commoners' foals. 8S belongs to Guy and Emma Sevier.
KH belongs to Kay Harrison.

Agisters' tail marks indicating their disctricts

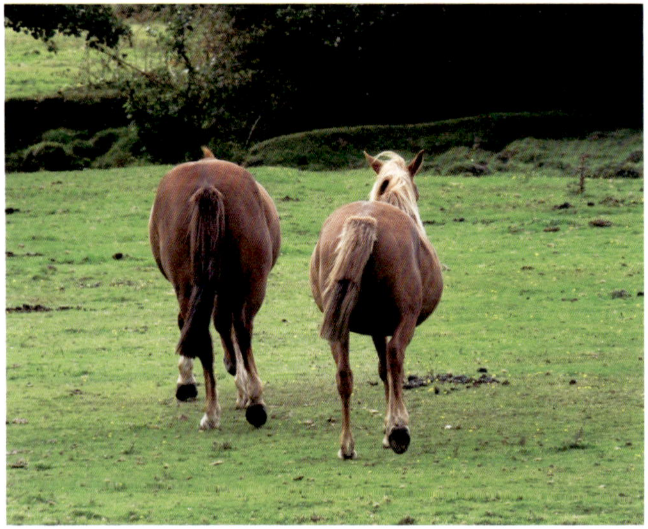

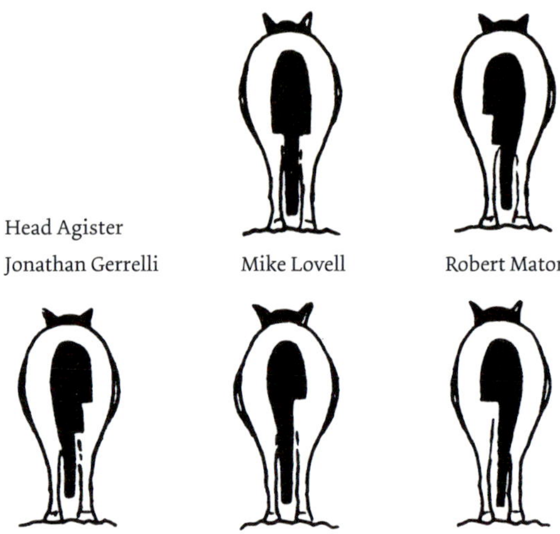

Head Agister
Jonathan Gerrelli

Mike Lovell

Robert Maton

Andrew Napthine

Peter Rix

Commons Animals

Above Ponies, in Mike Lovell's area, who have had their tails marked, 2005.
Opposite Agister tale marking in the pound with his special scissors, 2004.

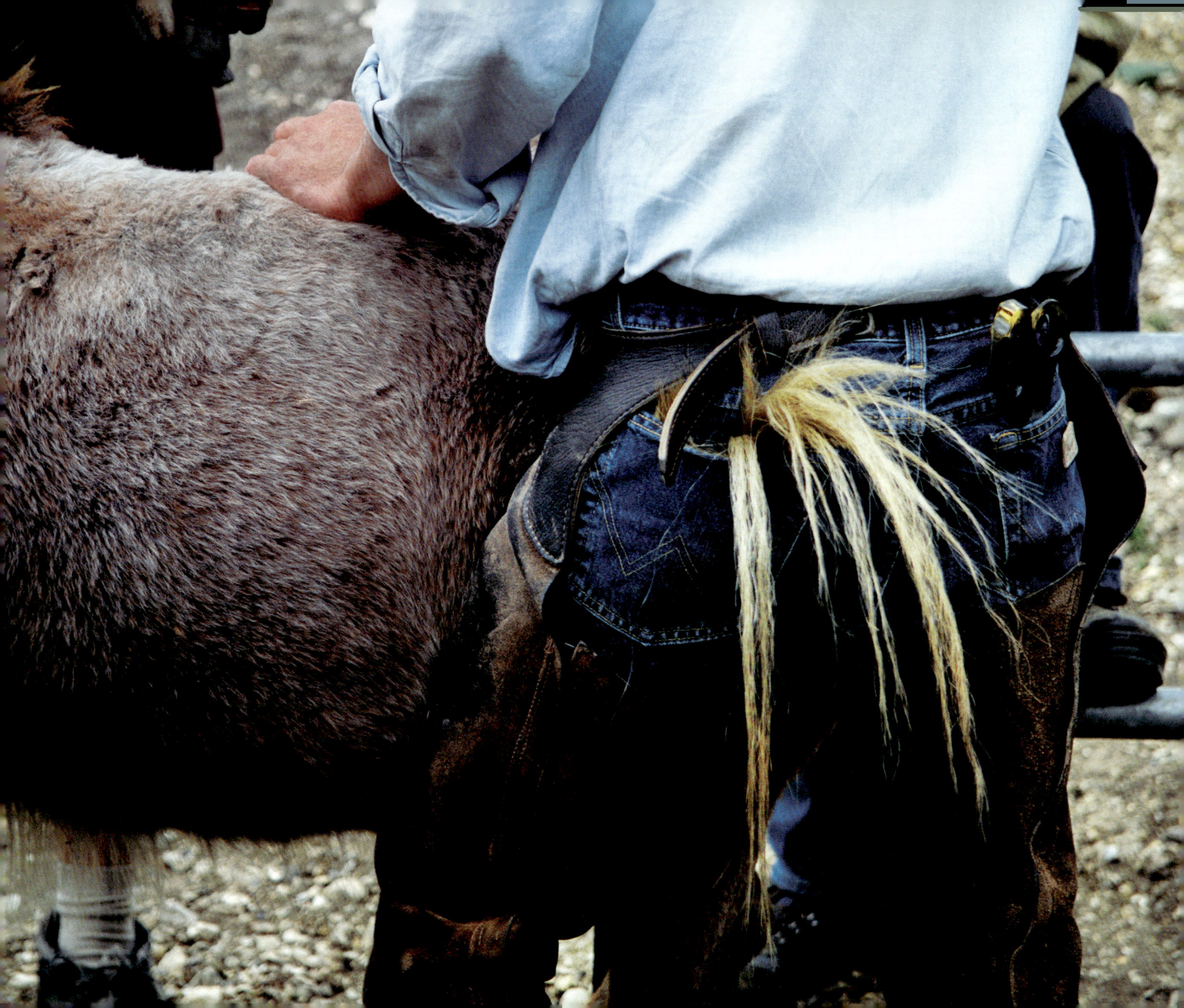

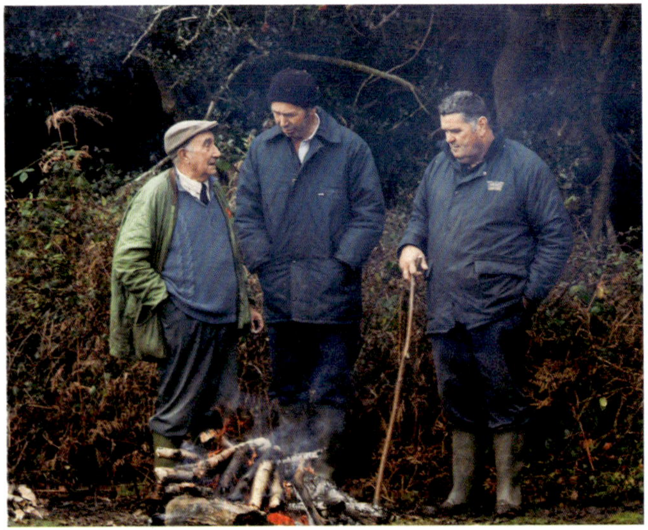

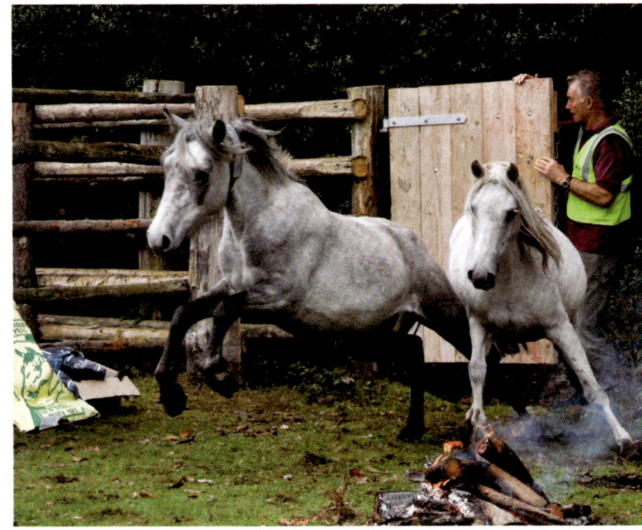

Above left (left to right) Les Maton, Kenny Rostagina and Jeff King keep warm by the fire at Holmsley, 2008.
Above right Mike Eccles lets two ponies back onto the Forest after they have been wormed and fitted with a fluorescent collar, 2007.
Opposite Commoners head back to the horse boxes after the drift at Ashurst, 2007.

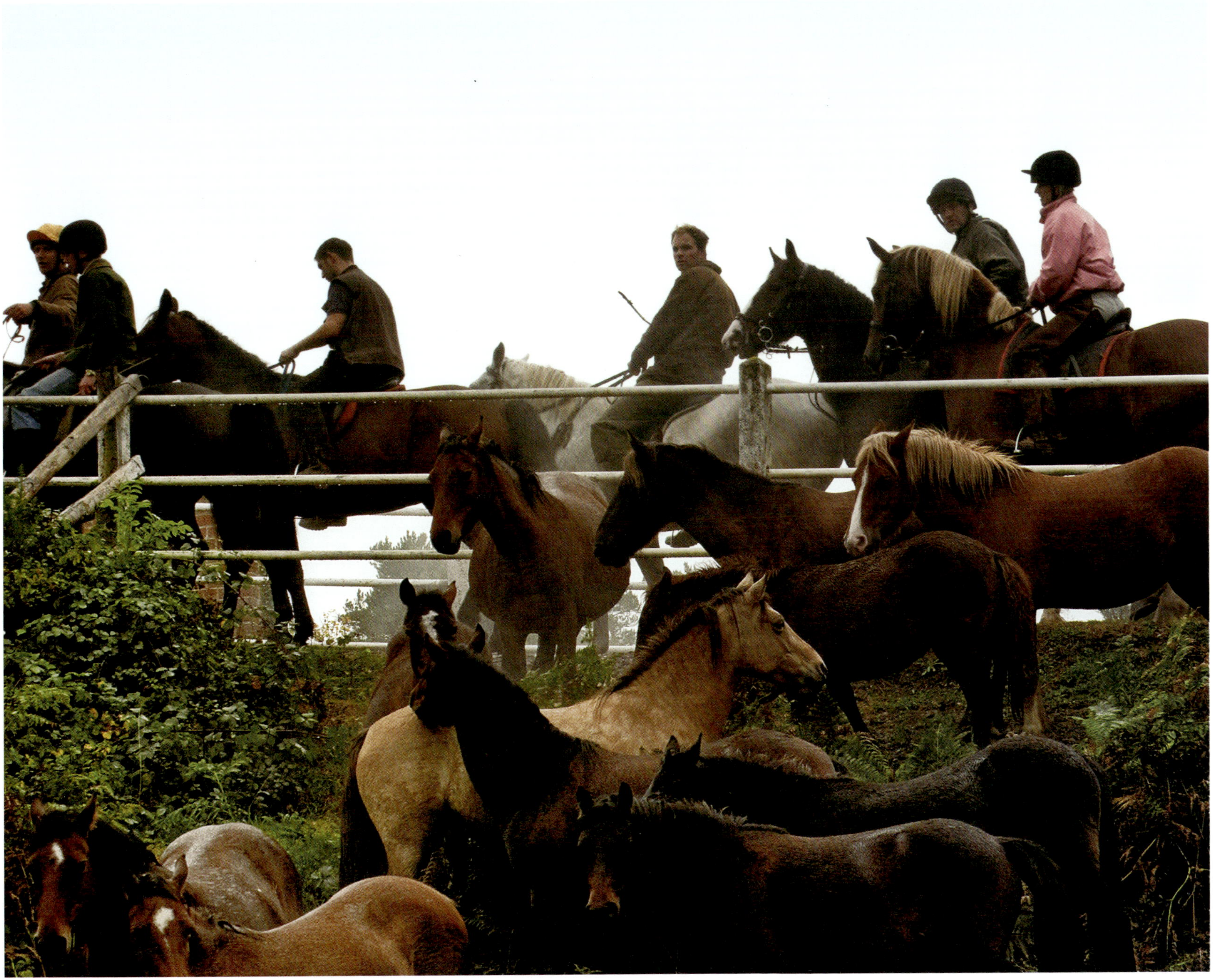

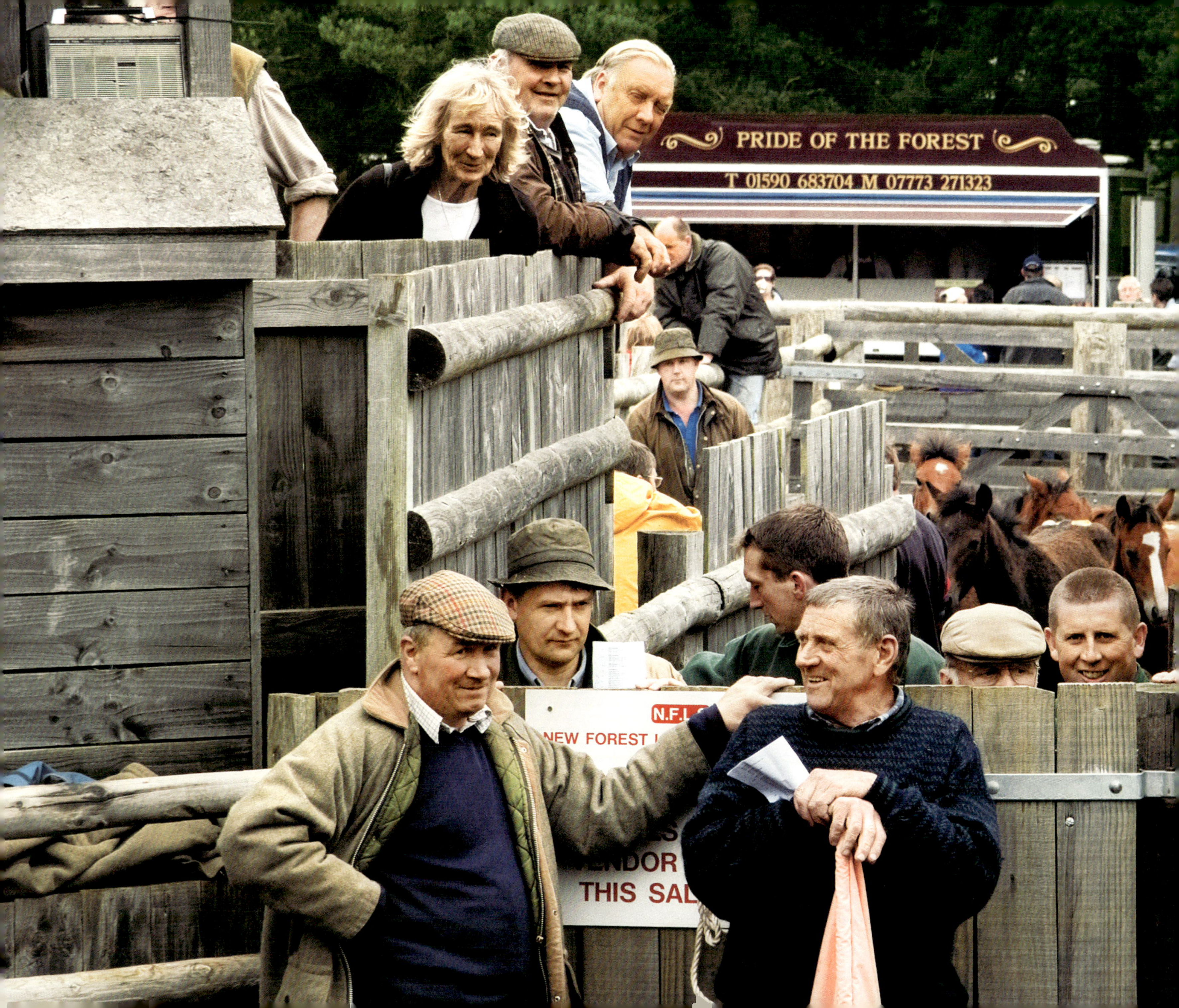
PRIDE OF THE FOREST
T 01590 683704 M 07773 271323
NEW FOREST

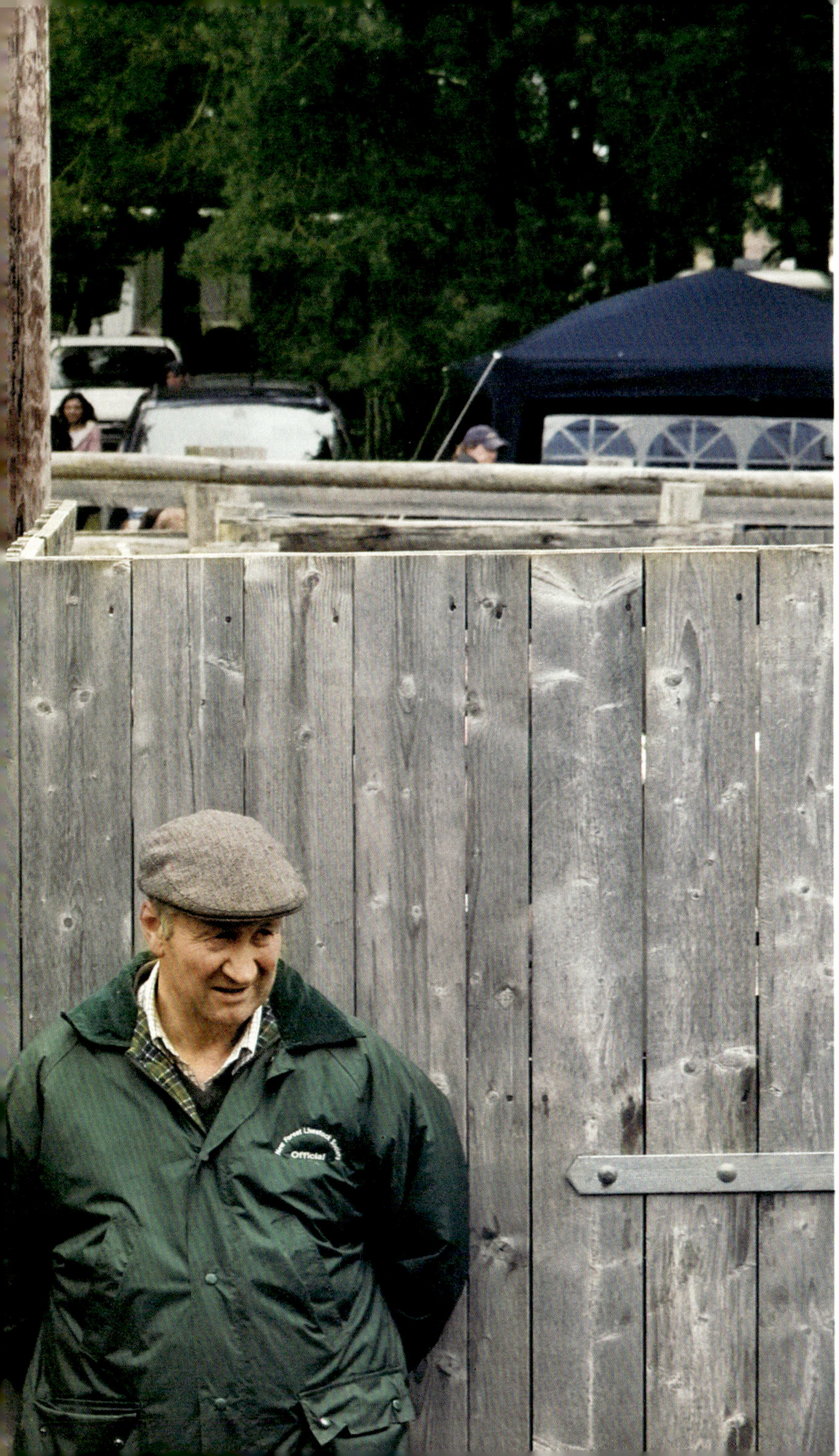

Beaulieu Road Sales Yard

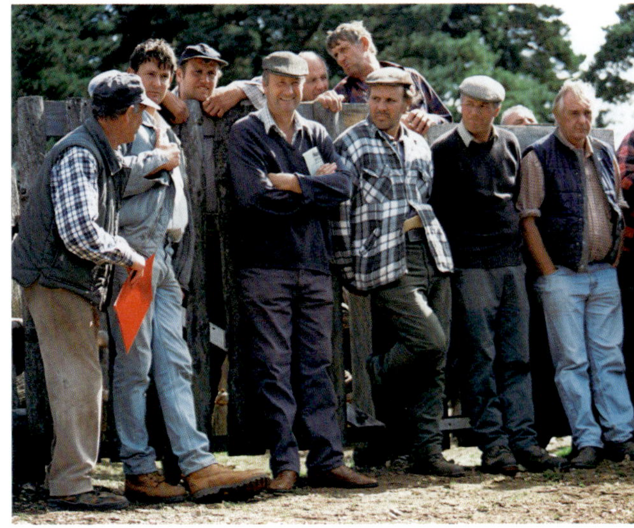

The Beaulieu Road Sales organised by the New Forest Livestock Society are held once a month during the drift season, with an additional sale in April or May for late foals. Ponies selected for sale by their owners only have a short distance to travel to the Beaulieu Road Sales Yard which is in the heart of the Forest. The sales have become well-established as the place to buy either broken ponies or unbroken feral stock and they attract buyers from far and wide. Entries for sale have to be made well in advance of the sale day in order for the details of the stock to make it into the catalogue. The sales days are very busy with horse boxes and trailers from all over the Forest bringing stock for the obligatory before-sale inspection by the vet and by the stewards of the New Forest Livestock Society. Any animal that is unwell, not fit to travel or immature may be rejected from the sale on inspection.

Above Commoners watch the action with interest at Beaulieu Road, 1999. *Opposite* Commoners selling their ponies at the Beaulieu Road Sales Yard, 2008.

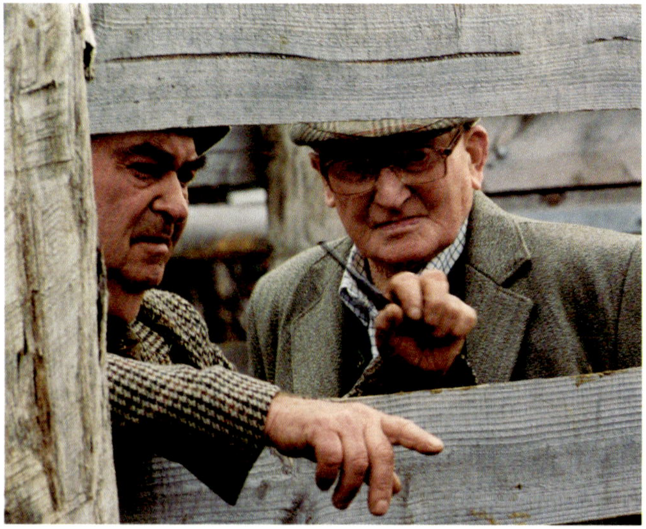

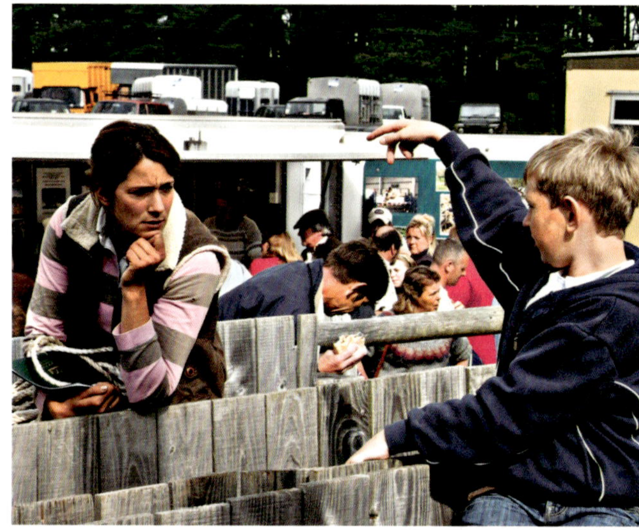

Above left Experienced commoners Henry Whitcher (left) and Len Mansbridge (right) discuss a pony at Beaulieu Road Sales Yard.
Above right Julian Pothecary relates the day's business to Beth Stride, 2008.
Opposite Jesse Winter points to the pony he wants out of the pen, 2008.

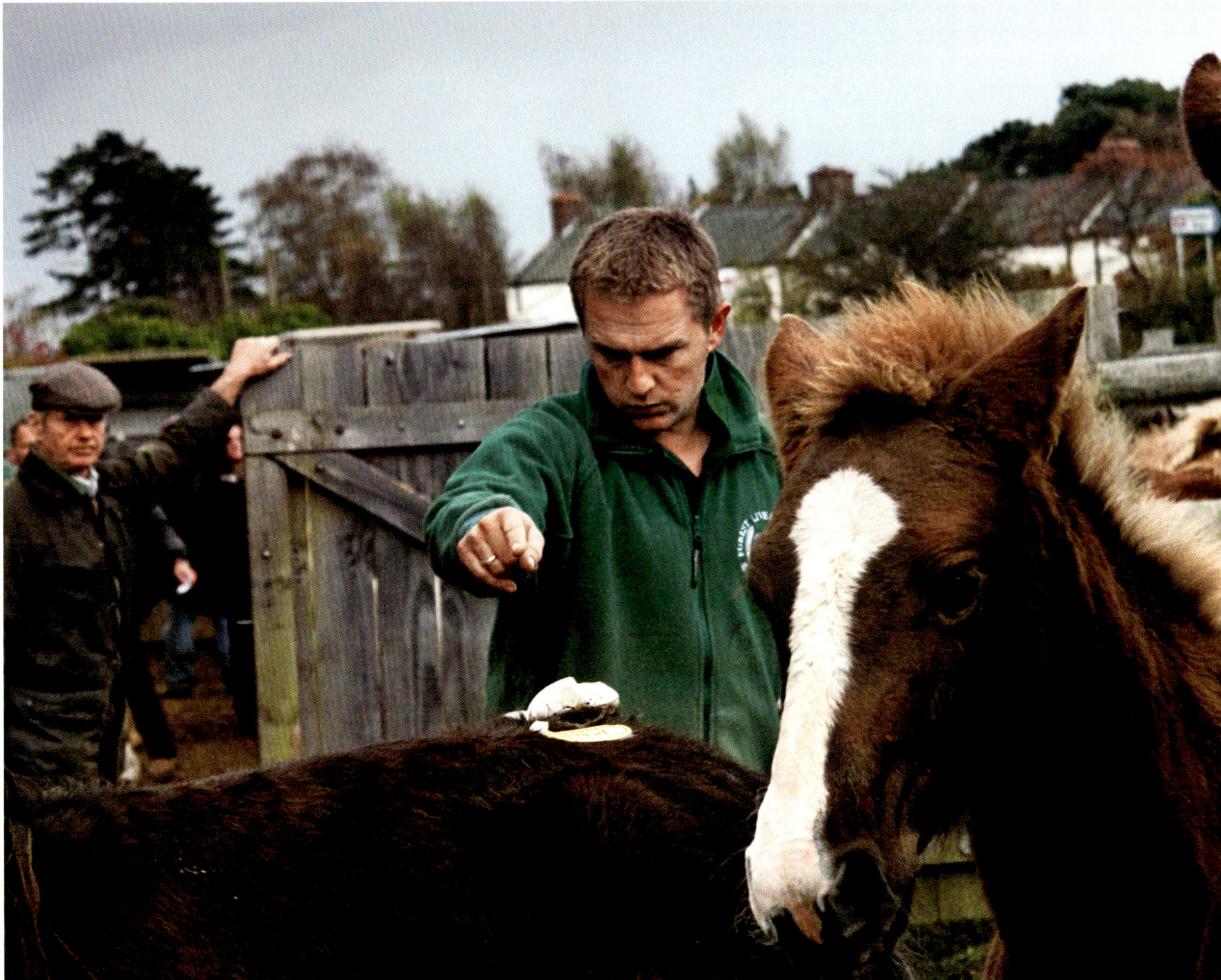

Once the ponies are declared healthy, they are given their sale number, sorted by size and moved to holding pens where they can be viewed by potential buyers. All the pens in the yard are made of Forest timber with gravel floors and are situated on the open Forest, ideal for holding semi-feral stock. Beaulieu Road is acknowledged as being one of the safest and most efficient sales yards in the country and its natural landscaping means it blends well with the surrounding countryside.

The auction prices are set in guineas. New Forest ponies are much in demand. Their hardiness and temperament make them ideal riding ponies and this means there is always considerable interest in the sales and stiff competition for good stock. The pre-sale Foal Show has done much to improve the quality and saleability of the stock. All fully-registered New Forest foals are eligible for entry and the show's prize winners fetch top prices at auction.

The sales are vital for the commoners and although some sell their stock privately, most sales of ponies go through Beaulieu Road. The sales are timed to ensure that foals can be weaned and sold immediately, as most commoners do not have the resources to keep their surplus stock. Older mares, stallions, geldings, non-registered ponies, Shetlands and donkeys are also sold at Beaulieu Road.

The traditional open air sales yard of 50 years standing was reconstructed in 2002, close to the original design. Forest organisations, supported by private funding, are now jointly backing a project to install water and electricity at the sales yard, and to roof the sales ring.

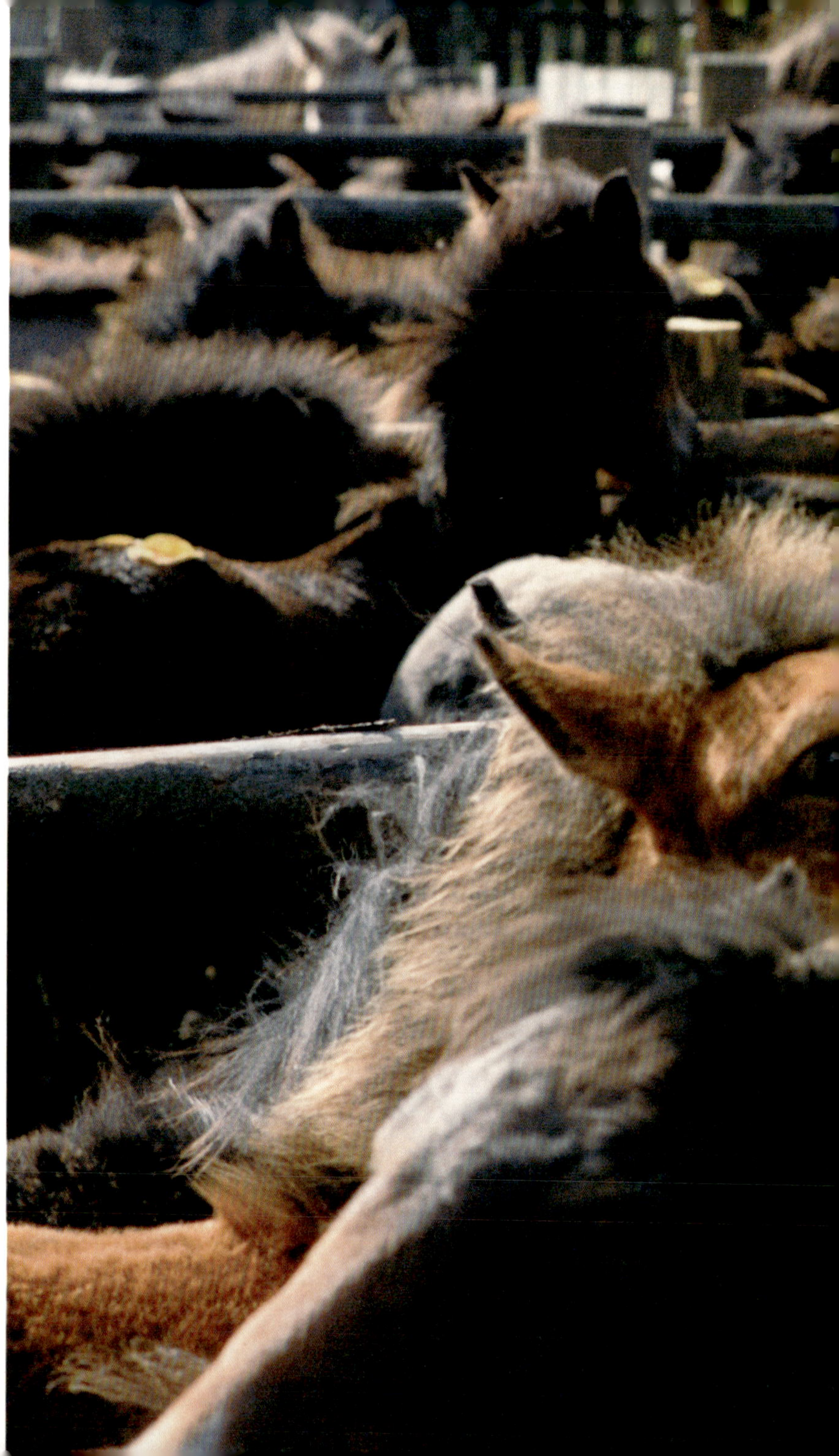

 Alan Ingram searching for ponies at Beaulieu Road, 1999.

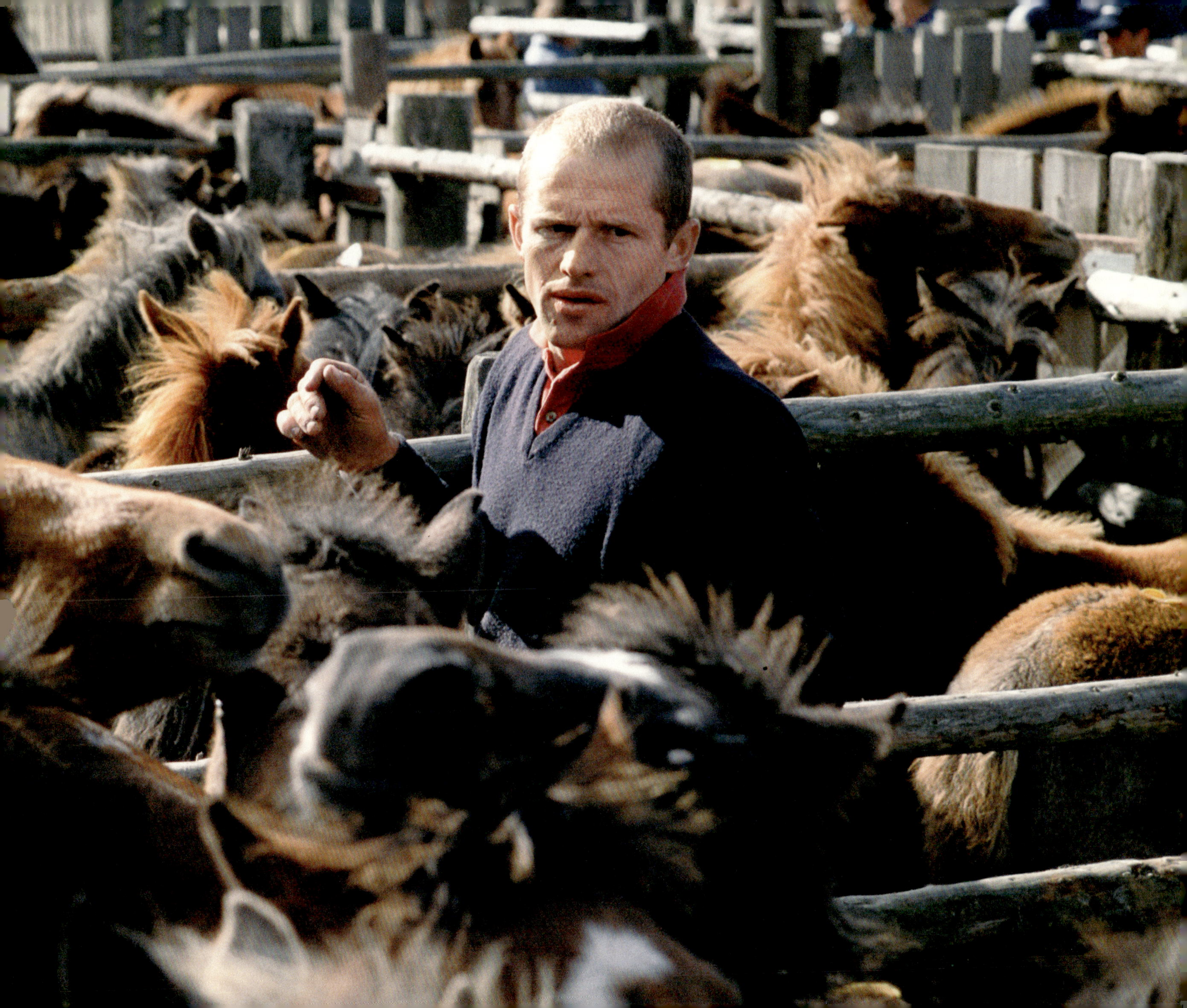

Shows

Many commoners like to show their animals. They have a great sense of occasion and enjoy the social side of shows. The New Forest Show, the largest of the year, takes place in New Park, Brockenhurst and is three glorious days of rural and agricultural tradition.

The first New Forest Show, a one-day event, was held in 1921. In 1978 the show grew to two-days and it subsequently became a three-day show in 1989. Held annually during the last week of July, the show attracts 100,000 visitors. It has an excellent reputation locally and nationally and is rated amongst the top five agricultural and equestrian shows in the UK.

There are many other shows held in New Park during the year. The first usually is the Young Farmers' Show, but probably the most important to the commoners is the New Forest Pony Breeding and Cattle Society Show, known as The Breed Show. This three-day show at the end of August celebrated its centenary in 2006. New Forest Pony owners travel from all over Europe to show their ponies – both Forest and stud bred.

Some commoners take their ponies and cattle to shows in neighbouring counties.

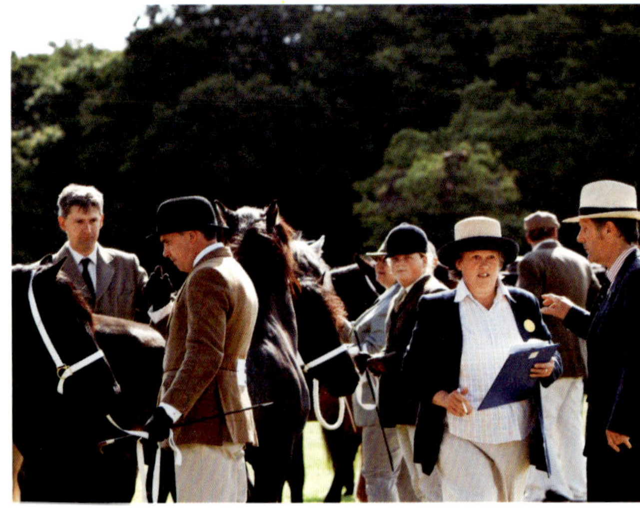

Above Commoners show their Forest Run stallions in the Breed Show, 2008. *Opposite (clockwise from top-left)* Matthew Pooley in the Young Handlers' Class with his pony Withybeds Wilson, 2007. Mike Kemish shows Judy Knight's champion bull Knightsway Paddy at her legendry Dexter sale, 2008. Robert Maton with Mallards Wood Goddess and foal, 2007. Lorrayne Blomfield showing her two-year old Simmental heifer Sway Topaz. Dorset Show, 2008.

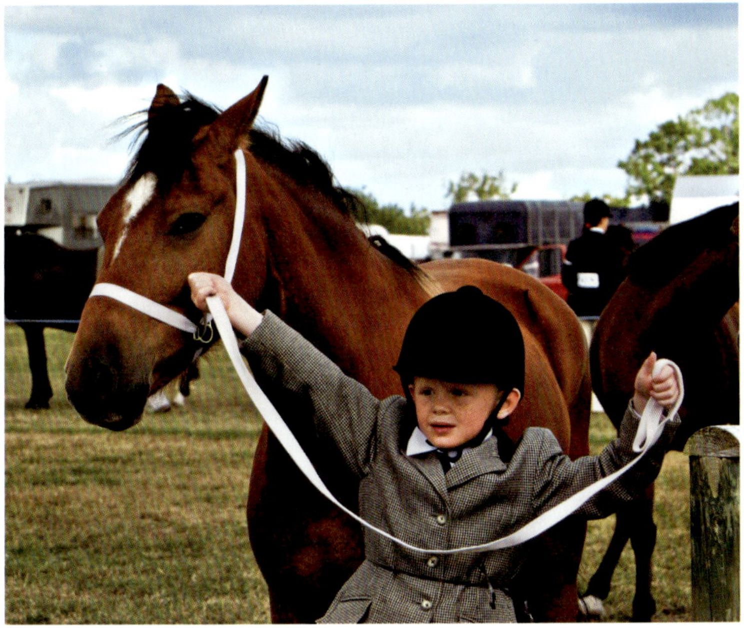
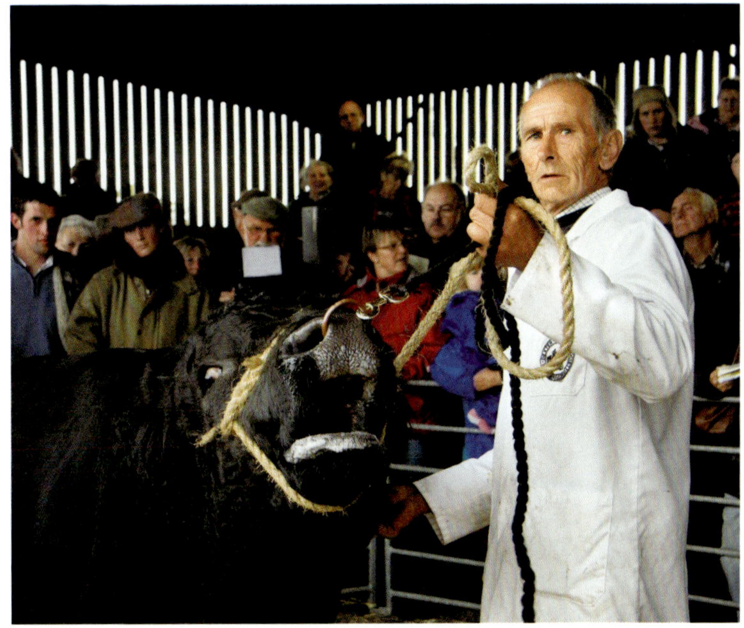
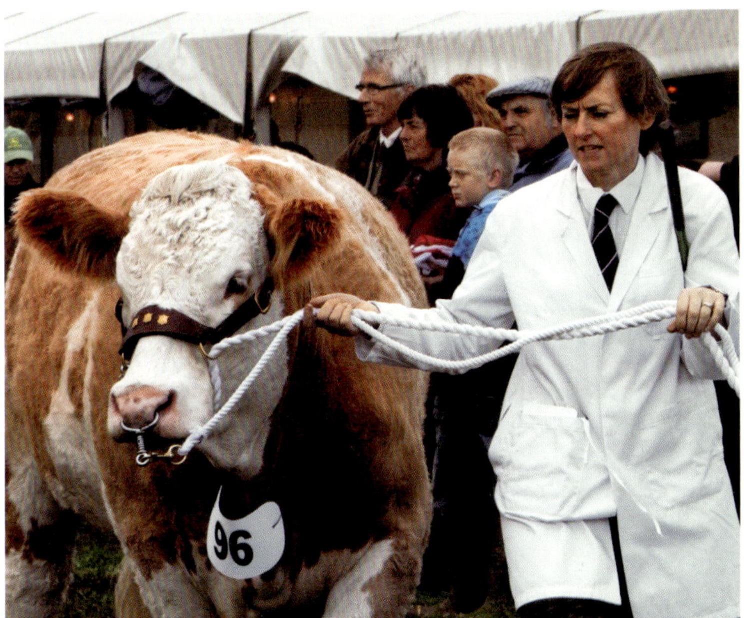
96
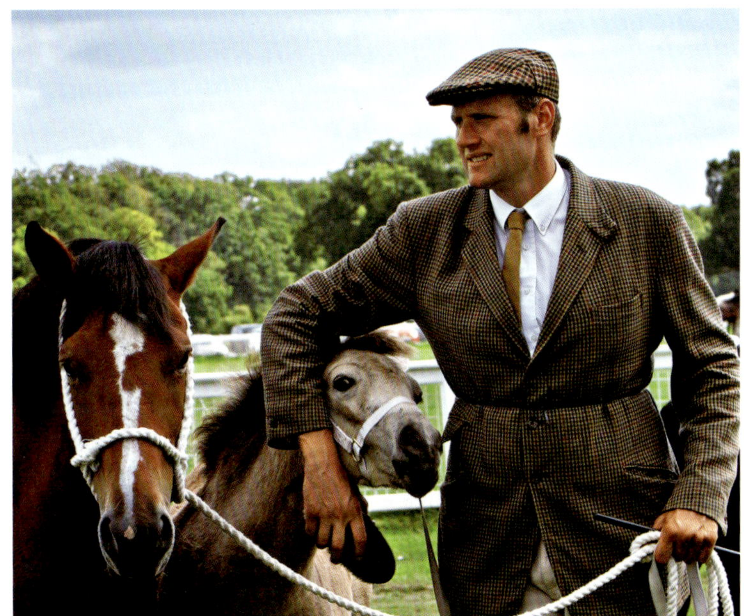

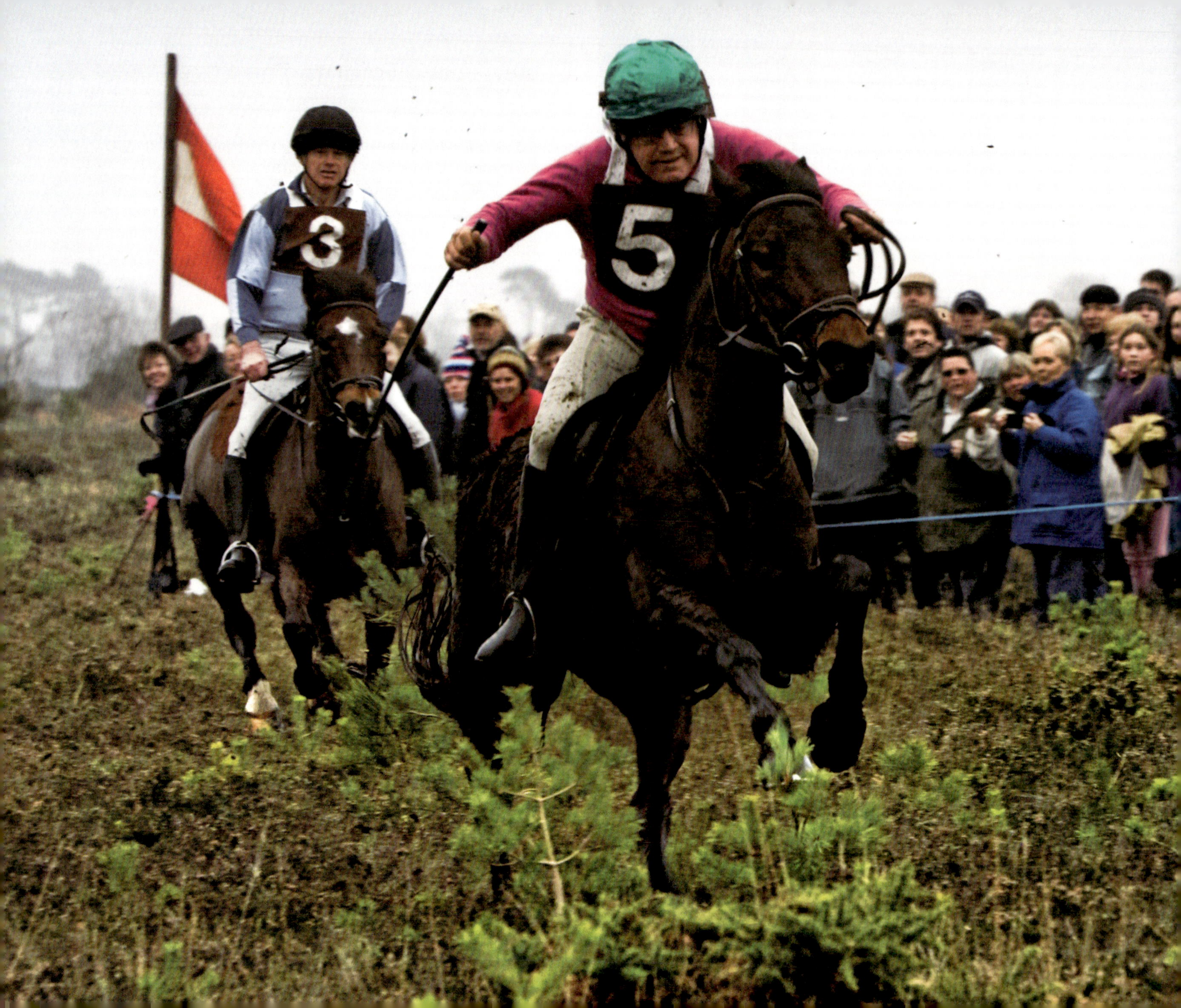

3
5

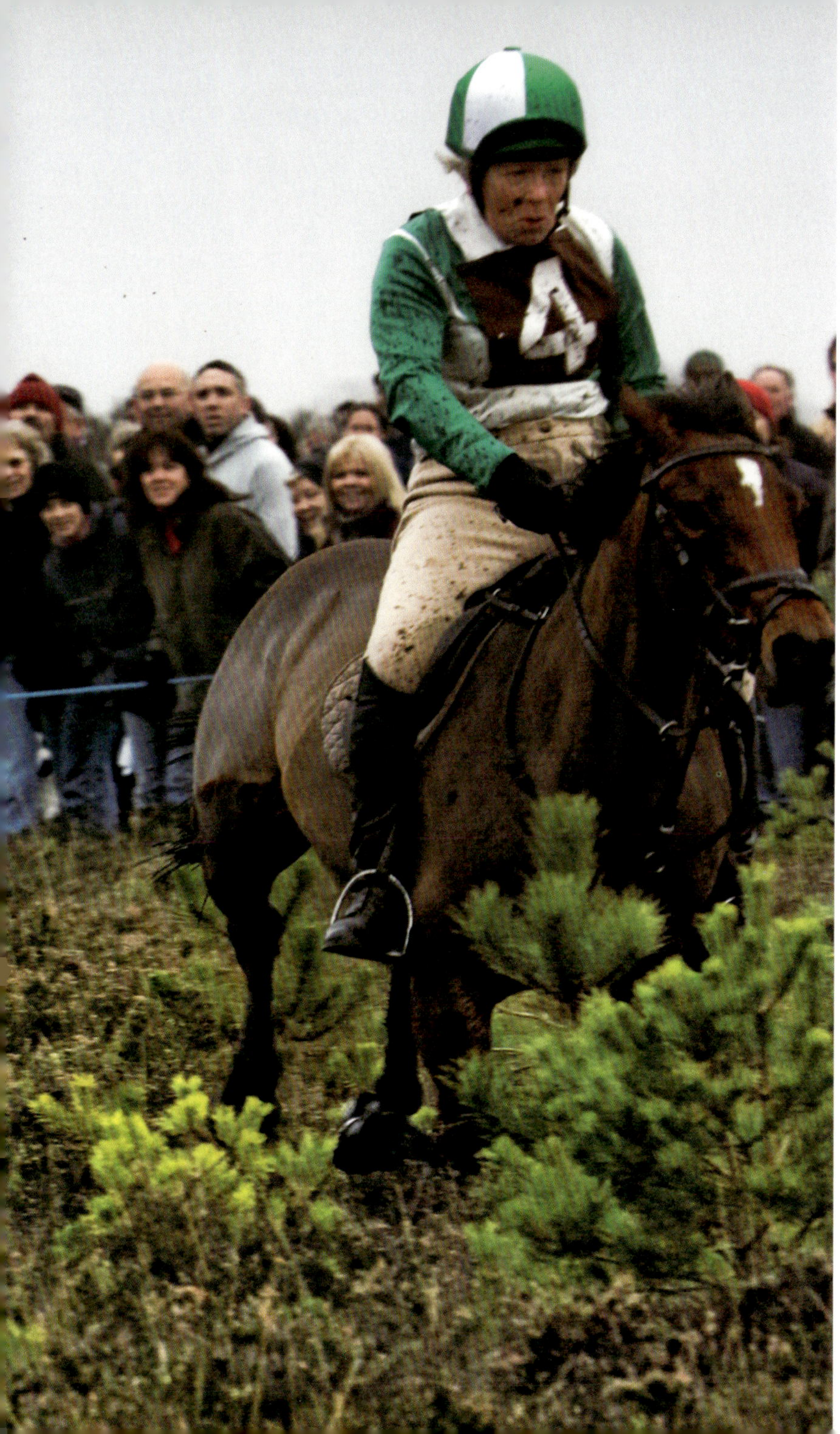

New Forest Point-to-Point

When the drift season is over, the highlight in the New Forest commoners' year is the Boxing Day Point-to-Point. It is the only true remaining point-to-point in the country without a set course and very little has changed since the first race in 1912. It is a hard race with seven or eight different classes and the training is rigorous.

On Christmas Day competitors find out where they are to meet, but are given no indication of the start or the finish. Each year the start and finish; which could be anywhere on the Forest, are selected by a knowledgeable commoner. On Boxing Day the riders are led deep into the Forest to the start. The finishing point of the race is then revealed.

The vet measures and checks the horses and ponies before the race starts. Everyone is aware of the hazards and the air is full of nervous tension. Most people navigate the race in a group, but some take a chance and go out on their own and, in the words of one young commoner 'what happens happens'.

The main course is three miles long, a little shorter for the juniors and veterans, and is designed to test the riders' skills and the Forest knowledge of both horse and rider. Bogs, thick woodland, rough heath land, slippery underpasses and many other hazards form part of every course and the finishes are often nail-bitingly close.

When it's over, all the weeks of exhausting evening training have been well worth it to the riders who had a thrilling and successful race. For those whose horse went lame on the day, or who fell off in a bog, there will always be next year. Whatever the weather, the point-to-point never fails to draw a large crowd.

Boxing Day is more important than Christmas Day to many commoners.

Jimmy Haynes on Gotton Petrushka wins the Veterans' Race for NF Ponies from June Whitham and Brian Ingram in the NF Point-to-Point, 2007.

Ecology of the New Forest

Commoners' animals have been grazing the New Forest for 1,000 years and this has produced its own peculiar habitat. It has a fragile ecology so it is important not to disturb the ancient ways.

The Forestry Commission is obliged to keep areas of grazing clear for commoners' animals. Controlled burning is an effective method of removing foliage and maintaining the low nutrient levels required of heathland habitat. The burning of specified areas each year creates a mosaic of diverse vegetation structure and habitats for many of the species for which the New Forest is well known. Dartford warblers can be found in patchy young gorse amongst the heather, whereas open ground free of dense vegetation is preferred by woodlarks, often to be found at recently burnt sites. The open heath is also an ideal nesting and feeding territory for the nightjar.

The sight of flaming heathlands can be alarming, but the fires are strictly managed and the wildlife benefits immensely. The burning takes place between 1st November and 31st March, which is determined by the 'National Heather and Grass Burning Code'. It is done when the ground is still wet in order to avoid harming roots or animals below the soil surface.

Today, huge numbers of people decend with their cars, caravans, tents, bicycles, games and dogs onto the Forest's fragile fabric. Recreation and tourism are of great economic importance to the Forest, but it has led to erosion of the land and disturbance of the wildlife. The National Park status means there are high levels of conservation on this unique landscape, but many continue to have ongoing anxieties that the increase in tourism creates considerable strain on the very fragile ecology of the New Forest.

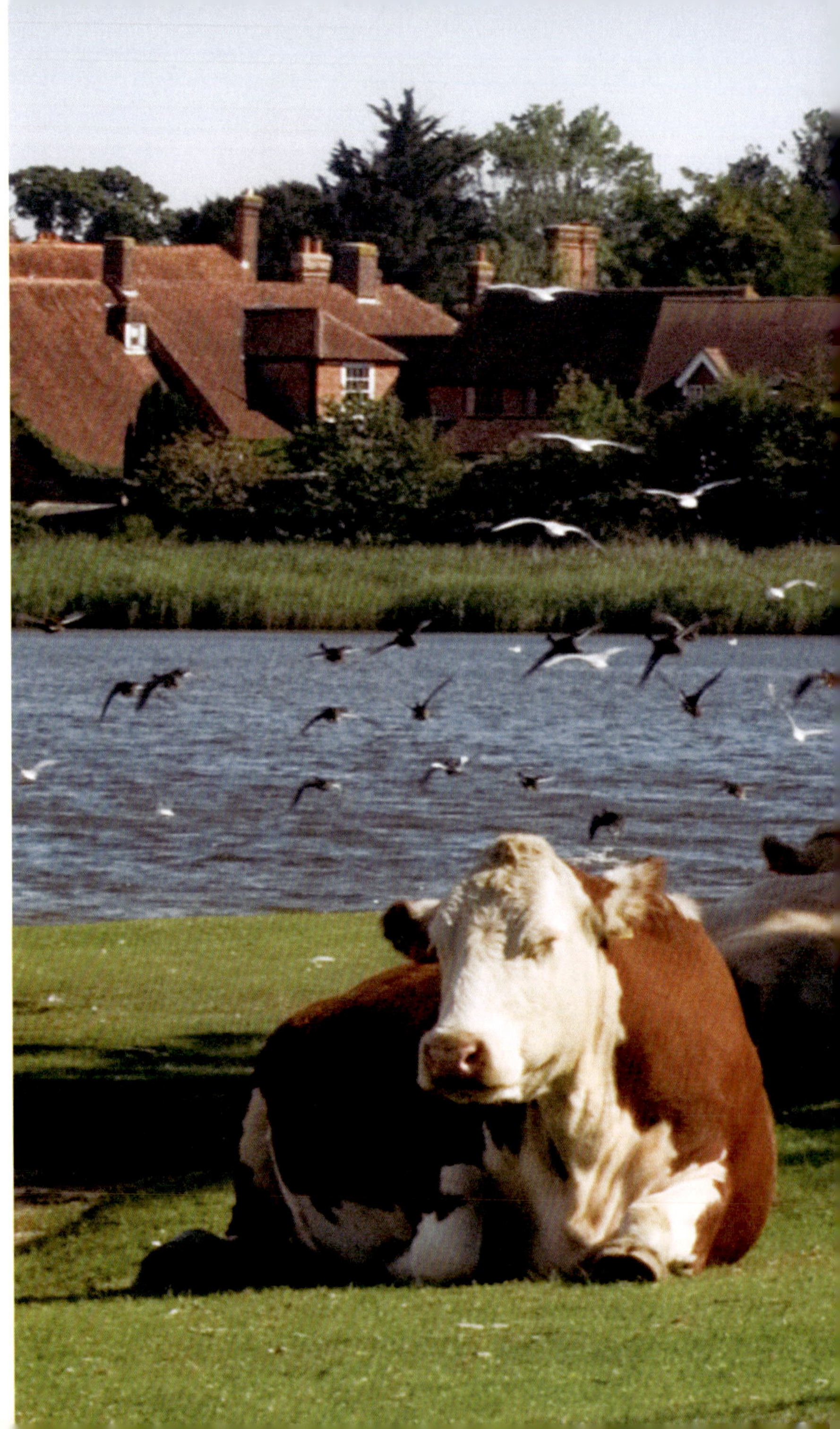

Cattle belonging to Steve White and Millie May, relax in the sunshine at Beaulieu. 2005.

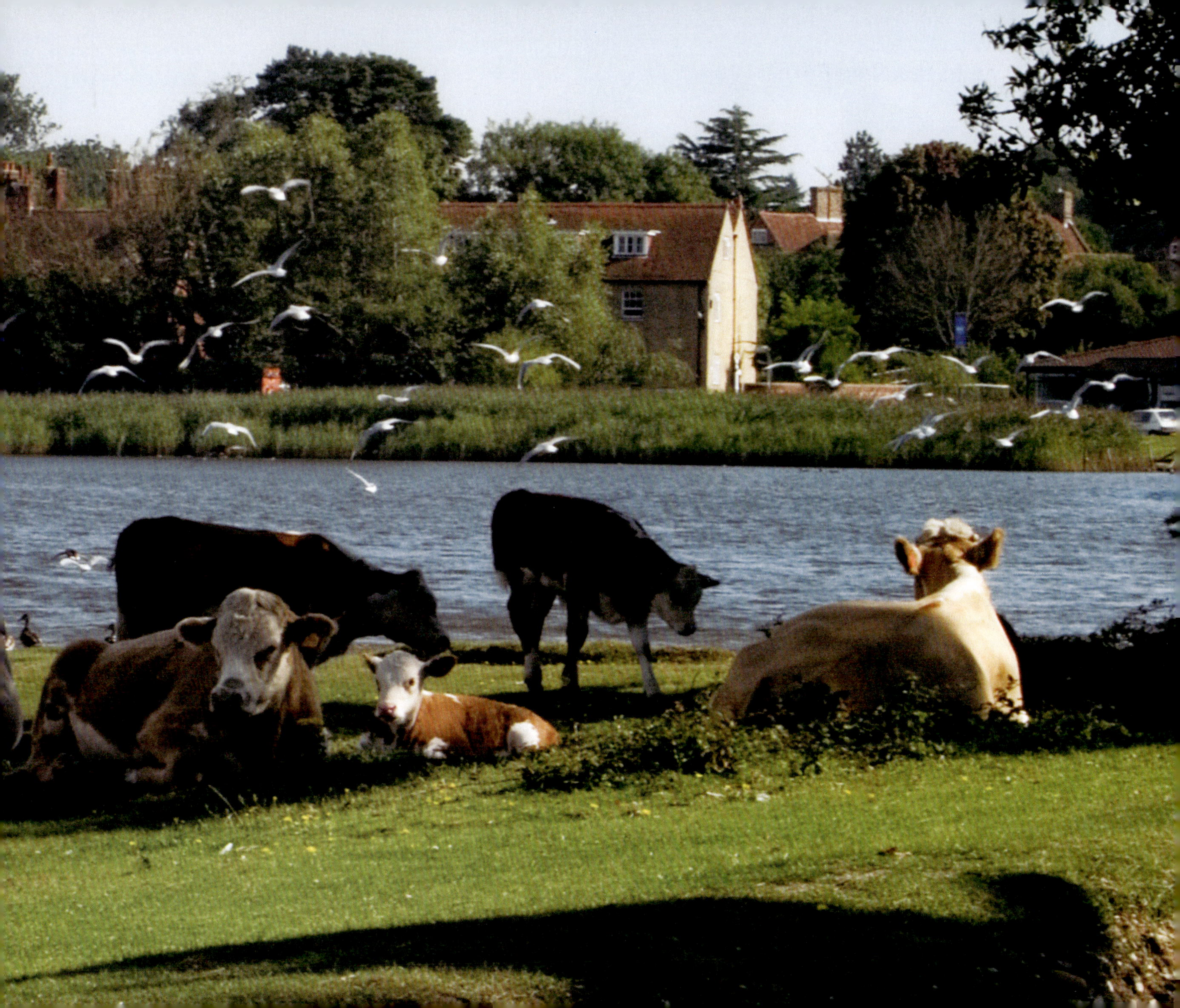

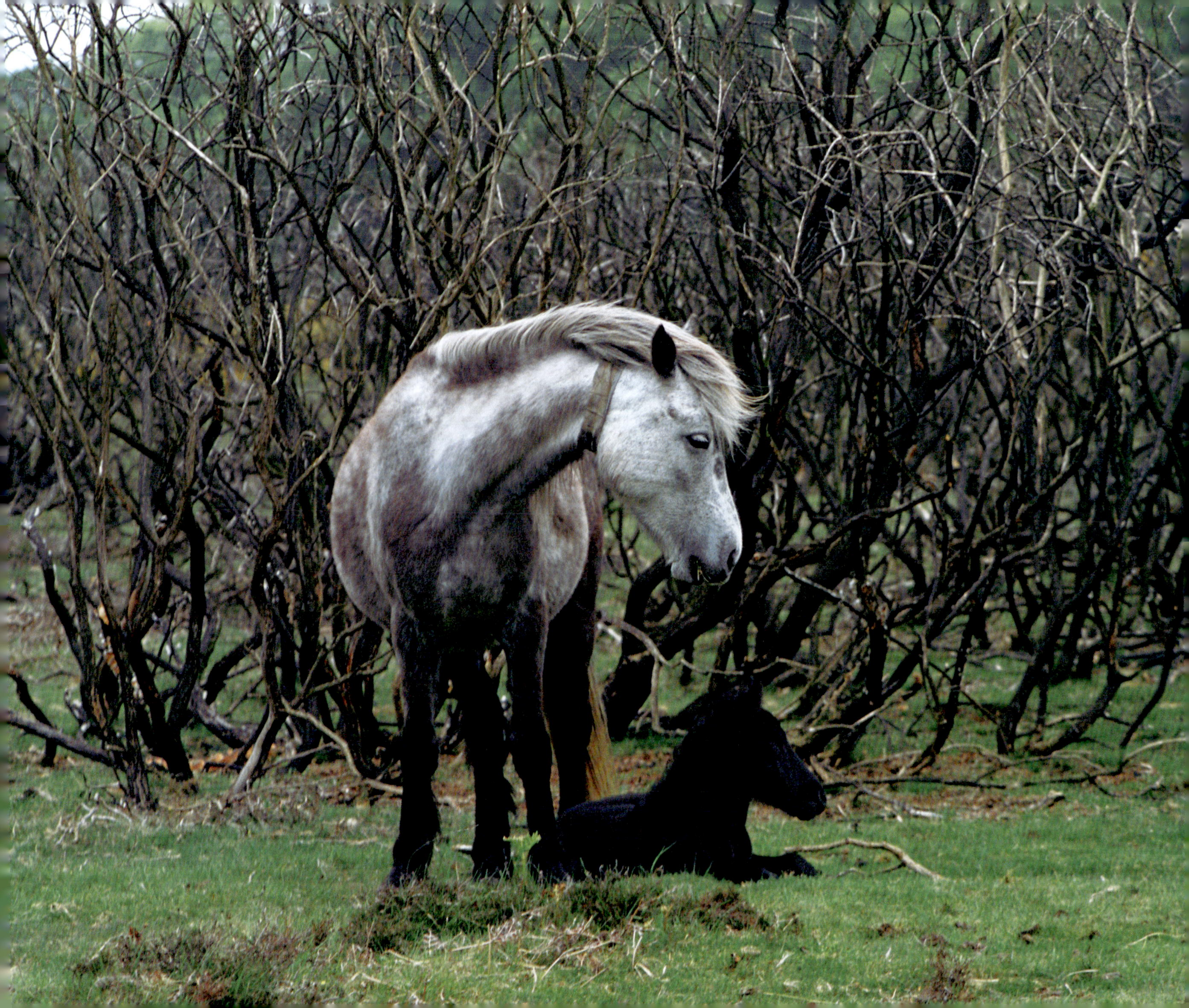

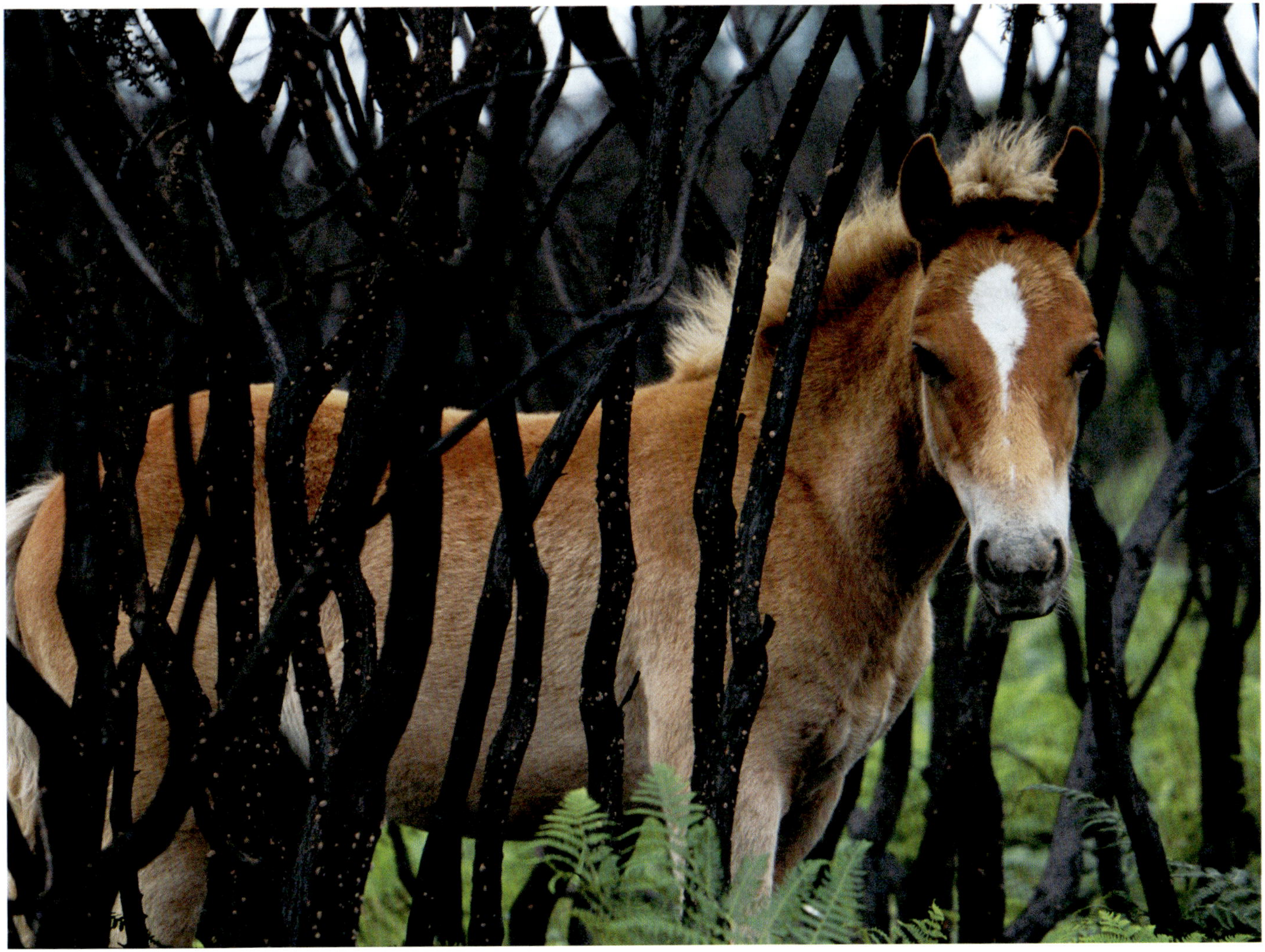

Opposite Canterton Blackberry (a graded NF mare) with her new-born colt foal, Black Jack Jones, in front of the newly burnt gorse, 2003. *Above* A foal peers out from burnt gorse where he has been browsing and grazing, 2004.

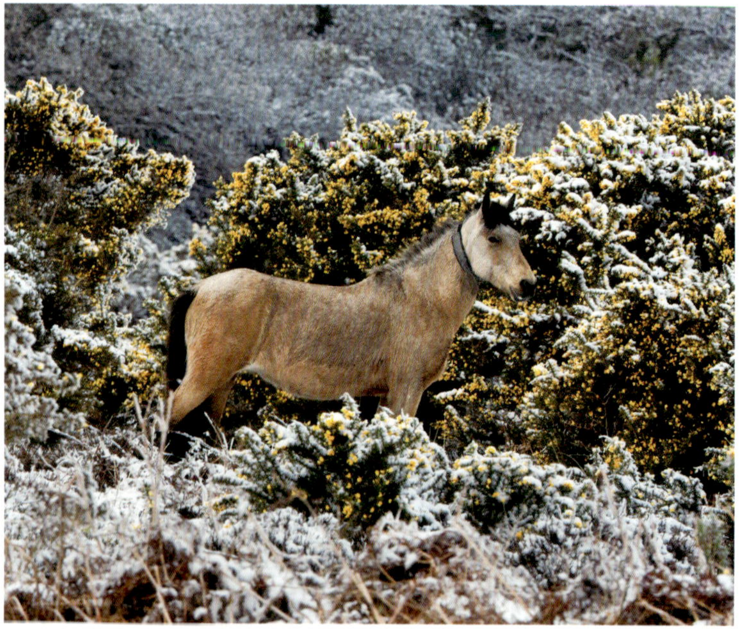
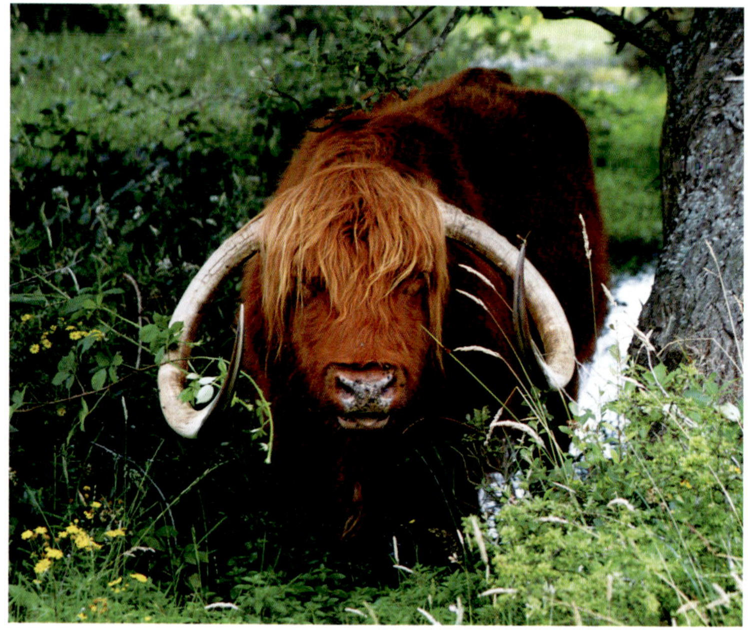
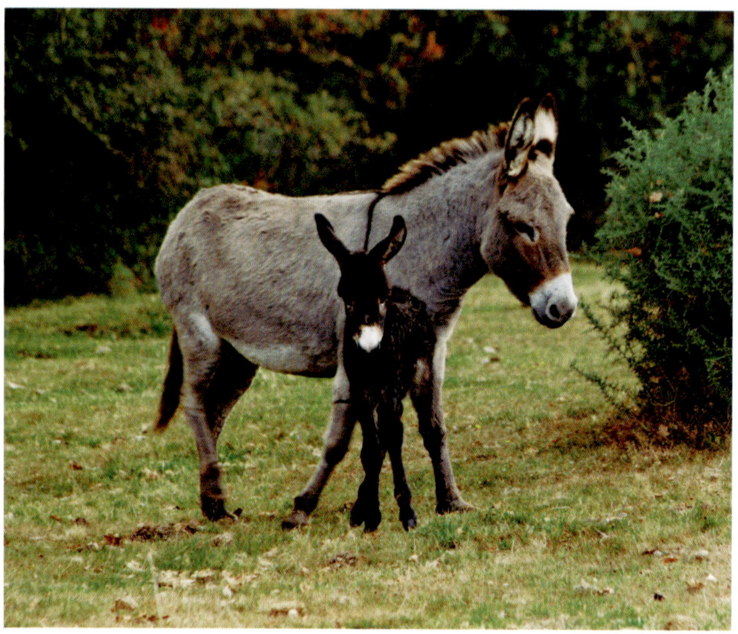
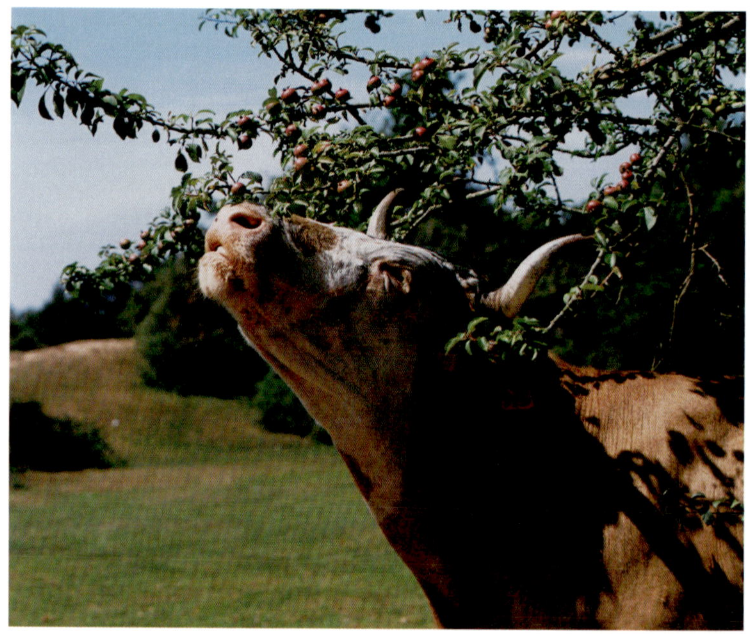

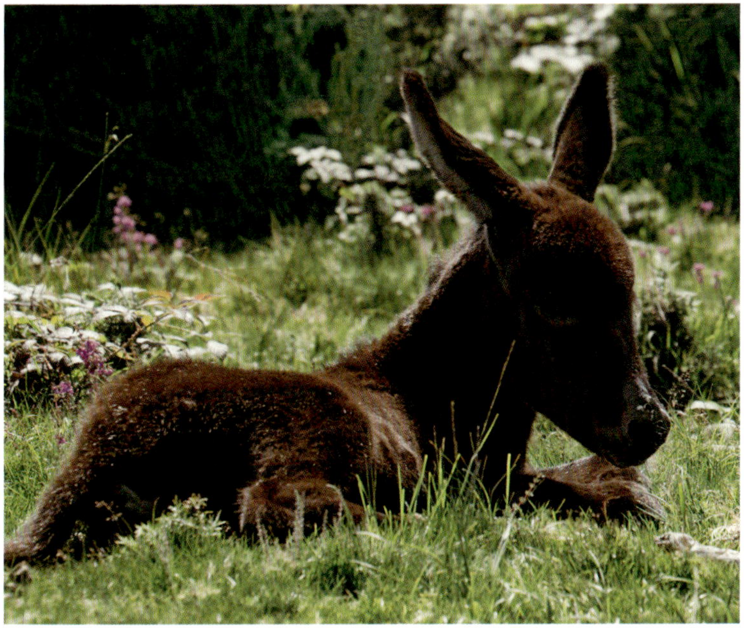
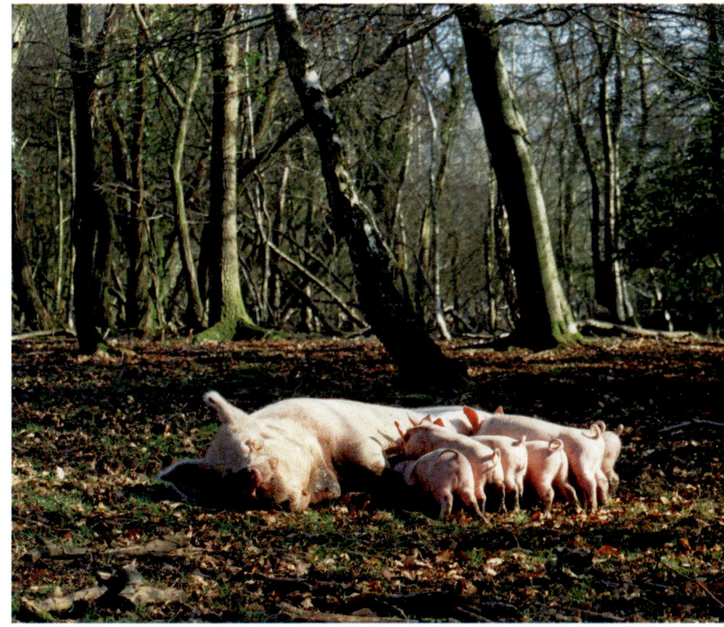
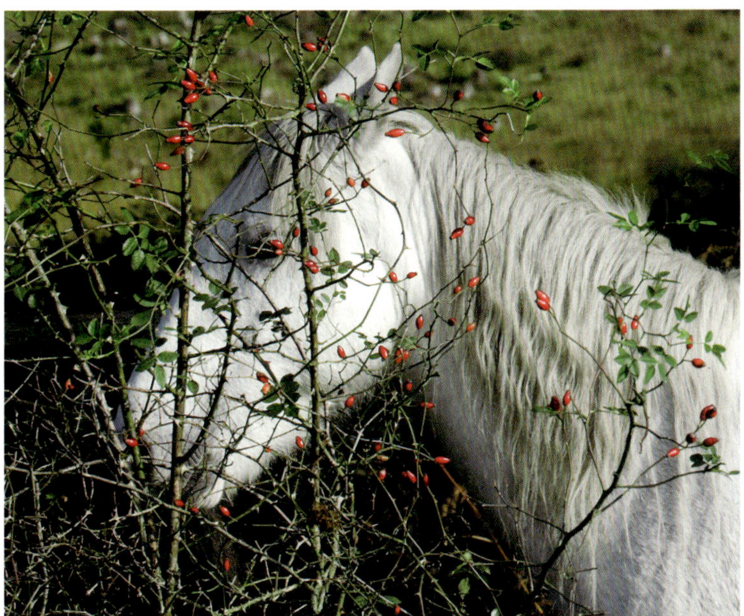
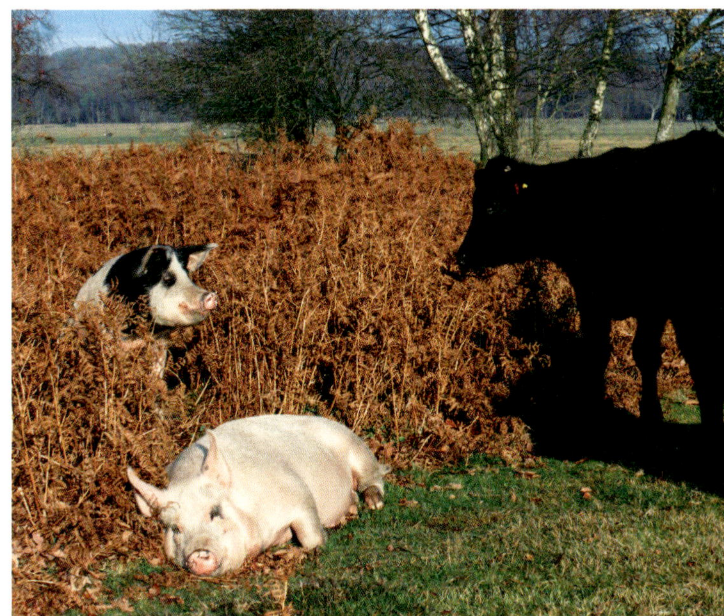

Rights of Common

The Right of Common of Pasture is the most important right, permitting the commoner to turn out ponies, cattle, donkeys and mules on to the common grazing. Those who wish to exercise their Right of Pasture do so by application to the Verderers' Clerk who confirms the existence of the right and allocates a brand for the animals. Once they have been branded, the animals may be turned out upon payment of a *marking fee*, which helps to finance the cost of employing the five Agisters who are responsible for supervising the stock on the Forest.

The Right of Common of Mast is the right to turn out pigs in the pannage season. Pannage runs for a minimum of sixty days in the autumn. Pigs are extremely important to the Forest because they eat acorns with no ill effects. Acorns eaten in excess may kill other grazing animals.

The Right of Common of Sheep permits the commoner to turn out sheep on to the Forest. There are very few sheep rights in the Forest and the right is rarely exercised these days.

The Right of Common of Marl permits the commoner to dig for a special type of clay that is used to improve agricultural land.

The Right of Turbary is the right to cut peat for fuel. Neither The Right of Marl nor The Right of Turbary is currently exercised.

The Right of Common of Fuel Wood (previously known as Estovers) is the right that everybody wants! Under this right, the Forestry Commission is obliged to give the commoner some free fuel wood, measured in cords. There are only about one hundred properties throughout the whole Forest to whom the Forestry Commission grant this right.

In addition to the six registered rights, some properties benefit from additional rights over the adjacent commons, such as the right to dig gravel or cut bracken for animal bedding.

Previous page left (clockwise from left) Didi van Hennik's mare stands in the April snow, 2008; Alan Gilbert's cow cooling off in a ditch of water, 2003; Steve White and Millie May's cow feeding on crab apples at Hatchett Pond, 2003; Raymond Bennett's jenny donkey and foal up on Penn Common, 2003. *Previous page right (clockwise from left)* The Byford's donkey foal, 2007; Mike Ralph's sow in the woods with her piglets, 2005; Dominic May's pigs meet cattle on Balmer Lawn, 2004. Pony in Wilverley pound, 2007. *Opposite* Stallion, Brookshill Royal, relaxing with one of his mares, 2008.

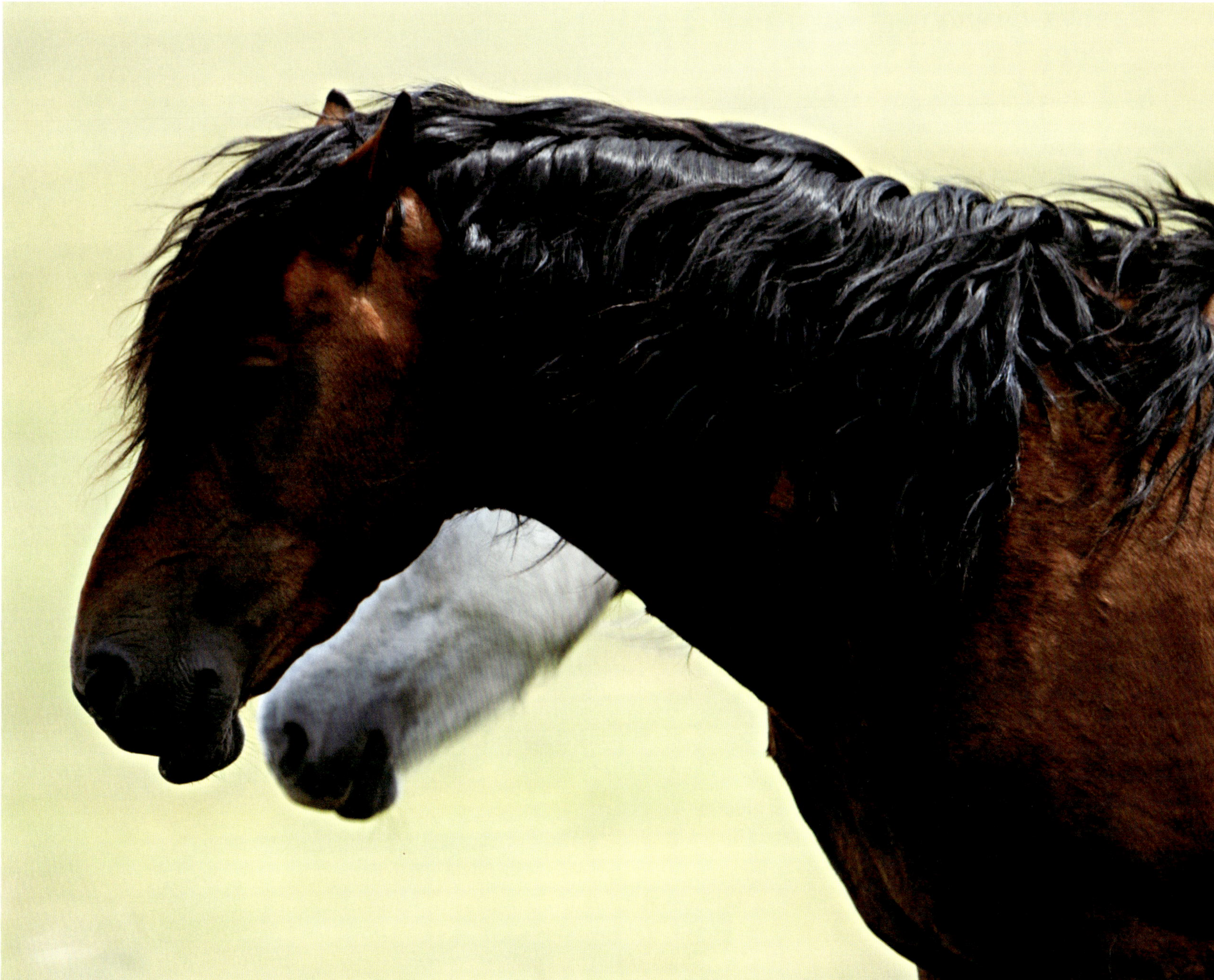

Glossary of Commoning Terms

Agister Agisters are unique to the New Forest. They are employed by the Verderers' Court and are responsible for the day-to-day welfare of the commoners' animals. There are five Agisters each of whom has an area of the Forest under his control. They organise the pony drifts in the autumn.

Blow-up A term used by commoners to refer to a pony which is being colthunted and suddenly runs out of steam.

Bottoms A name for valleys, where commonable animals spend much of the night feeding on the coarser herbage.

Branding Iron An iron about 80cms long usually made by a blacksmith. On the end of the iron there is a letter, a number or a combination of the two, selected by the owner and approved by the Verderers, to be his or her brand mark. Ponies are branded on the left side, usually in the saddle area, but sometimes on the shoulder. Cattle are now freeze branded or marked with an ear tag bearing the owner's brand.

Browsing Besides grazing ponies, cattle and deer also eat vegetation off the ground: holly, gorse, ivy, young saplings and the leaves of mature trees. This is known as browsing and supplements the animals' winter diet.

Browse Line A very visible line, usually about 2 metres above the ground, where Forest animals have eaten the vegetation. Sometimes the browse line is higher than usual as a result of deer standing on their hind legs to reach higher food.

Clipped Out The hair of an animal is clipped short at the appropriate spot to receive the imprint of the branding iron. An experienced commoner holds the red hot brand in place briefly and does not harm the animal's flesh.

Clipping Out Scissors Curved scissors to cut the hair without damaging the skin.

Colt A commoner's name for a pony of any age or sex.

Colthunting The art of rounding up individual ponies required for a particular purpose.

Cord Wood A stack of firewood 4ft × 4ft × 8ft (105cm × 105cm × 210cm) used in the supply of wood for commoners' fuel 'rights'.

Drift An old term for the rounding-up on horseback of considerable numbers of ponies or cattle. The Agisters organise the drifts in the autumn all over the open forest.

Driftway A track or lane running between enclosures.

Estovers A Forest 'right', also known as the 'Right of Common of Fuel Wood'. Only about 100 properties in the Forest have this 'right'. The Forestry Commission is obliged to give these commoners a certain number of cords of wood. The allocation comes with the property.

Furze Gorse. Pronounced 'fuzz'

Haunt When ponies or cattle are turned out to graze on the Forest they normally will settle down and live quite happily within a radius of two or three miles; hence they are said to 'haunt" a specific area.

Holms A clump of holly trees.

Keeper Employed by the Forestry Commission, they control the deer population and carry out annual culls. They also oversee the general day-to-day activities on the Forest. There are 12 Keepers.

Lane Creeper Before the Forest was fenced and gridded, animals strayed down roads and lanes well boundary, outside the Forest where the roadside grazing was attractive. They were called 'lane creepers'.

Marking Fee The fee (£20) paid by the commoners to the Verderers for each animal turned out on the Forest. The fee is collected by Agisters who ensure each animal is tail marked and branded.

Marl A Forest right which permits the commoner to dig for a special type of clay that is used to improve agricultural land, or for the building of cottages. Not currently executed.
Mast A Forest right which entitles the commoner to turn out his pigs during the pannage season.
Open Forest, Open Waste or Crown Land The commonable lands of the Forest in Crown ownership.
Pannage A season of a minimum of 60 days in the autumn when the acorns fall on the ground.
Passage A path across a bog, or valley mire, such as 'Matley Passage' or 'Admiral Murray's Passage'.
Perambulation A grid and fence line, erected under the 1964 New Forest Act to enclose common land. This stops the commoners' animals from straying into adjoining villages and towns.
Portable Pound A portable heavy sectional enclosure used for drifts.
Pound A timber enclosure (or corral) built at strategic points in the Forest to facilitate the rounding up of commonable animals.
Presentment A request, complaint or announcement made in public before the Court of Verderers.
Runs Similar to 'haunts'. It can be said that a pony 'runs' in a specified area of the Forest.
Shades Ponies and cattle group together in summer in certain spots where wind currents deter flies. Often they stand head to tail and flick their tails across the face of their neighbour. Some shades marked on 1909 Ordnance maps are still in use today.
Shelling Refers to a pony changing its teeth. Between the age of two and three, the milk teeth give way to adult teeth.
Small Commoner A practising commoner deriving a small part of his/her living from the Forest.
Sucker A foal.
Sucked Yearling A yearling which is still feeding from its mother.
Tailing Occasionally used by commoners to catch foals and yearlings the commoner gallops alongside the quarry and grasps the tail to slow it up thereby enabling a halter to be fitted.
Tail Marking Every commonable animal turned on the Forest has to have its tail cut to an identifiable shape by the Agister to denote that its marking fee has been paid to the Verderers. This mark also designates the area of the Forest where the owner lives.
Turn Out To turn out is to depasture animals on the Forest i.e. to set them free on the Forest.
Turbary An old Forest 'right' attached to a holding entitling the commoner to cut peat to fuel his/her particular holding. Not currently exercised.
Verderers of the New Forest A corporate body which oversees commoning on the Forest. It employs five Agisters and holds an open court ten times a year.
Walkers Commoners assisting at a drift on foot.

The Future

The New Forest Commoners' Defence Association was founded in 1909 to defend the rights of commoners, quite literally. There was increasing conflict between the spreading fringe Forest population and the commoners' animals, who frequently strayed outside the Forest and were impounded. The residents of the new suburbs did not like or understand animals and the countryside, and this hostility put great pressures on the commoners.

The Association's main purpose is to support the right of commoners to turn their stock out on the open Forest. It has always insisted on full consultation with the commoners over issues that concern them. Amongst the battles the Association has fought on behalf of its members are:

- In the 1920s the NFCDA actively petitioned the Office of Woods (now the Forestry Commission) to improve drainage on the open Forest.
- In 1936 the NFCDA paid for the installation of telephones in the Agisters' homes, to enable them to reach animals injured or killed in road accidents.
- In 1949 the NFCDA pressed for the introduction of the Tuberculosis Testing Scheme in the Forest. By 1956 the Forest became the first area on the English mainland where all herds had gained attested status on a voluntary basis.
- In the 1960's the Association supported the campaign to grid and fence the Forest that resulted in an act of parliament in 1964.
- In 1990 a uniform 40 mph speed limit was put in place on all unfenced New Forest roads. The NFCDA had vigorously campaigned for this, together with other Forest organisations.
- During the 1990s the Association developed the successful reflective collars for ponies to increase visibility at night.

In 2007 a Young Commoners group was formed within the NFCDA and in 2009 a Colts Council (under 16) was established.

President Jeff Kitcher plays an active role in maintaining commoning traditions. He has owned ponies since his birth in 1942 at Furzey Lodge where he still lives. He was given his first pony by his father and has still got 'one or two ponies out on the Forest today who are descended from her'.

Elected a Verderer in 1991, his family timber business gives him sound understanding of the Forest, and combined with his specialised knowledge in practical management of livestock, he exemplifies what is best about the Court.

Appointed an MBE in 2002 for Services to Commoning and the New Forest, he regards the honour as being for 'commoning and for all the commoners who do so much hard work to keep the Forest the way it is'. The Commoners' Defence Association works with the Verderers, alongside the National Park and the Forestry Comission, to protect the Forest from the impact of visitors, and of course from those with a commercial approach to the Forest.

Following the retirement of their Chairman, retired Head Agister Brian Ingram, the NFCDA appointed a new Chairman, Graham Ferris, who rears cattle and sheep on his smallholding, runs ponies on the Forest and hunts regularly with the New Forest Hounds. Together, with a strong committee and the young commoners, they will protect the New Forest for their children, grandchildren and of course the rest of the nation.

We owe an enormous debt to Lord Arthur Cecil who recognised the need for the New Forest Commoners' Defence Association a hundred years ago, which has ensured the maintenance and protection of Forest as it is today.

Jeff Kitcher with his grandson Josh and Ernie Mansbridge at Iron Bridge, 2007.

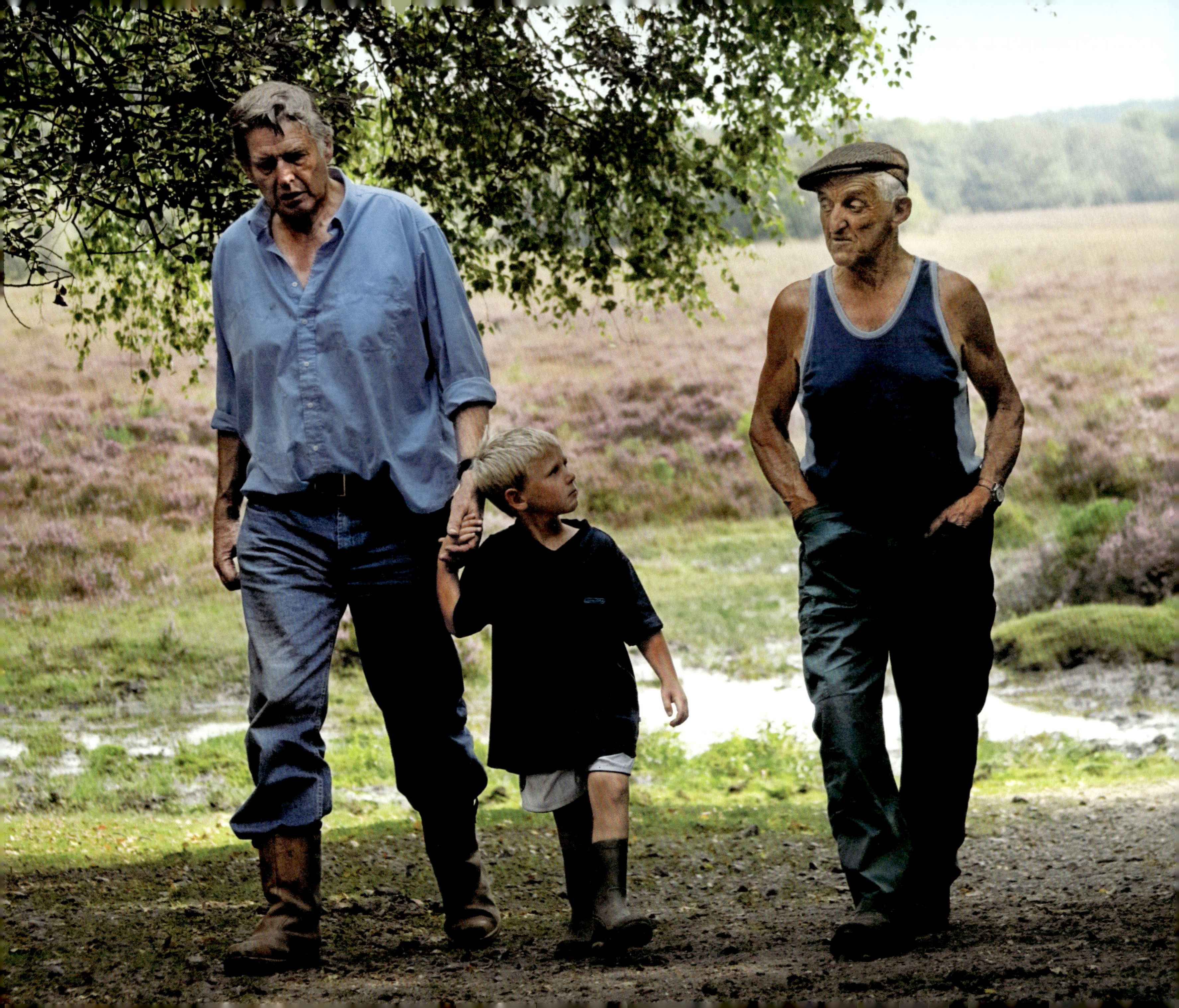

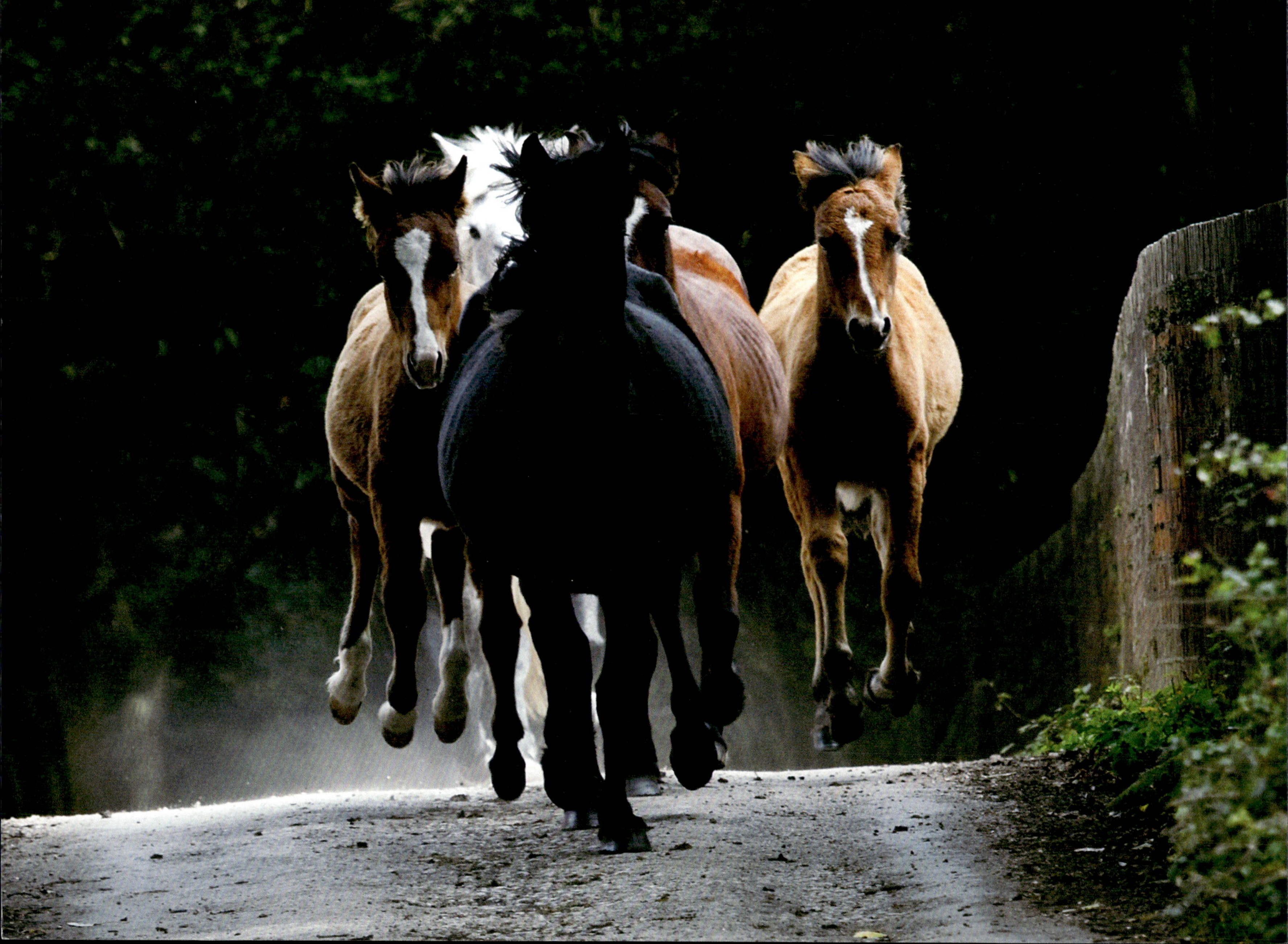

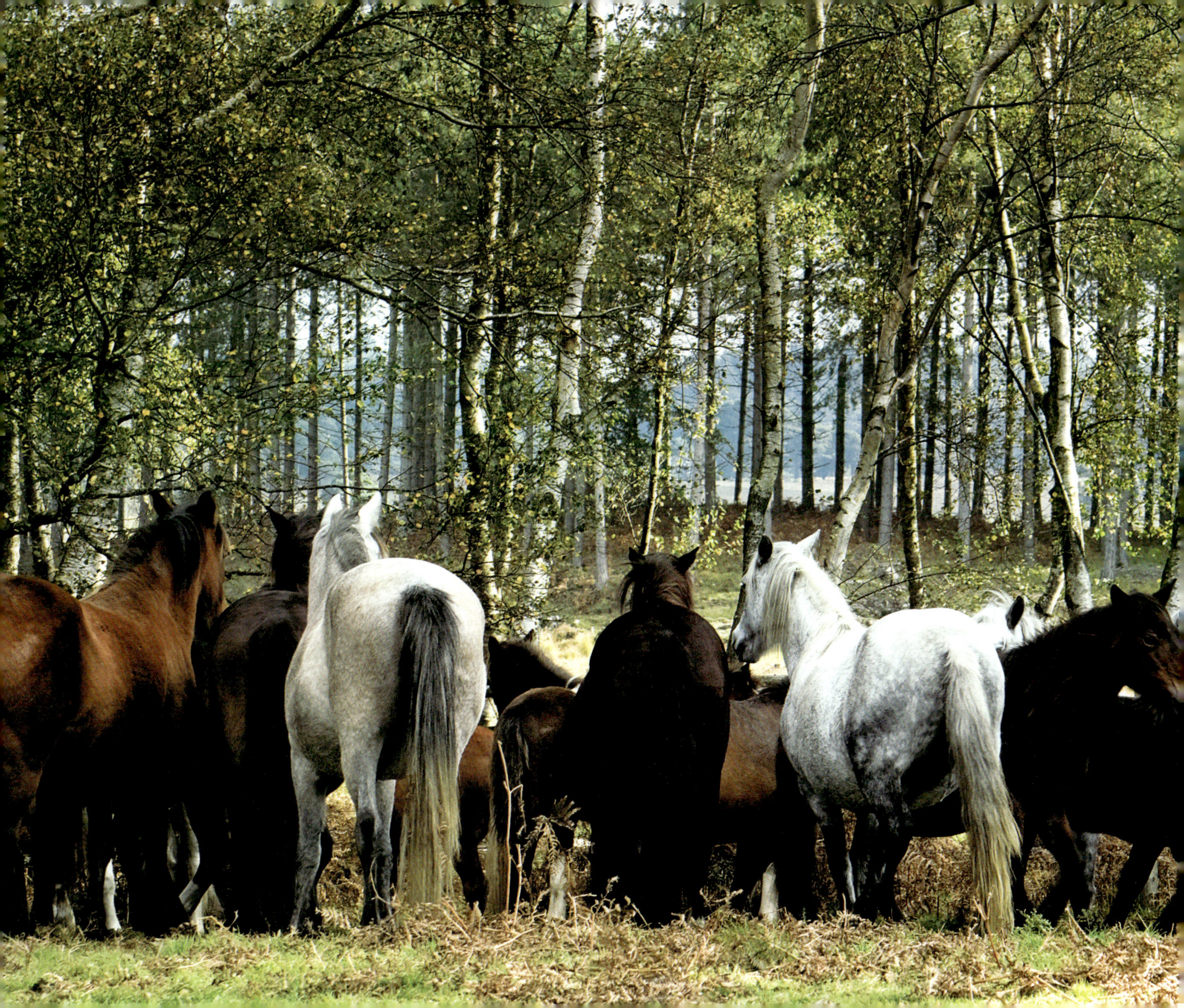

Acknowledgements

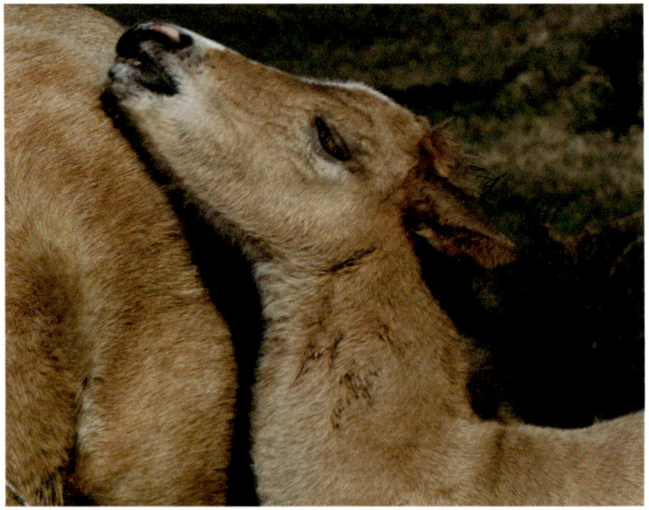

During the making of this book I relied on many Forest people including Official Verderer Oliver Crosthwaite Eyre and elected Verderers Tony Gerrelli, Jeff Kitcher and Anthony Pasmore; the Agisters, especially our own Agister Robert Maton; Sue Westwood the Clerk to the Verderers and her assistant Sally Cardwell; Jayne Pothecary and the commoners who enthusiastically searched their attics for historical photographs; the friends who cared for my animals when I was taking photographs; Arthur and Margaret Tucker, Catherine Pope and family; colleagues including Philippe Achache, Christopher Cormack, Dave Raven, David Reed (Photoshop expertise), Patrick Ward, special thanks to Julian Calder for his publishing inspiration; Langham Browne for storing the book; the medical team (traditional and alternative) who have held my back together; Dr. Sarah Jarvis, Dr. Neil Fraser, Dr. Gertrud Mander, Miss Jane Bridges, Mr. John Nixon, Professor Anthony Wright, St. Margaret's Physiotherapy Centre, Robert Lever (cranial osteopath), Beryl Tollady (Alexander), Marion Watt (Bowens).

I would like to honour some of those who are no longer here: my first husband Hugh 'Eddie' Eddison and my mother Paddy Fear; commoners Diana Halford, Freda Harding, Ralph Hayward (who dismounted from his horse to pick me up when I fell off on a drift and broke my back), Roly Ralphs, David Stagg, Don Stephens, Frank (Buzz) Terry, Brian Tillyer.

I thank Anthony Pasmore for 'Verderers of the New Forest: A History of the Forest, 1877–1977', and his many 'Forest Notes' in the Lymington Times. I could not have produced my book without his vast knowledge.

My heartfelt thanks and appreciation to Stu Smith and all at SMITH Design. It has been their encouragement, ideas and sound advice that has made this book possible.

Finally my gratitude and thanks yet again to my husband Richard Harris-Jones who has supported my work throughout.

The author and publisher gratefully acknowledge the permission granted to reproduce the copyright material in this book. Every effort has been made to trace copyright holders and to obtain their permission for the use of copyright material. The publisher apologizes for any errors or omissions in the list below and would be grateful if notified of any corrections that should be incorporated in future reprints or editions of this book.

I thank the commoners and institutions for their historical photographs: Tony and Eileen Gerrelli, Brian and Marion Ingram, Jeff Kitcher and Christine Drodge, Dionus Macnair, Peter and Val Penny, Tom and Joyce Penny, Richard and Caroline Stride, Richard Reeves and Peter Roberts in The Christopher Tower New Forest Reference Library, Hampshire Museum Services, Hampshire Record Office (105M93/4/11,105M93/2/25, 105M93/3/12 and HPP31/067).

Opposite New Forest mares and foals coming over Coxhill Bridge, 2008.
Above One of the first Forest foals born on Setley, 2009.
Following Ponies resting in the pound at Wilverley, 2008.